Step Out Of Fear and Into Faith

Step Out Of Fear and Into Faith

Everyday Lessons Learned from a Global Pandemic

CARLA GREEN

Dedication

This book is dedicated to the church, the bride of Jesus. You will and will always be essential to the world. Jesus sacrificed and died for you. Romans 8:19, "The entire universe is standing on tiptoe, yearning to see the unveiling of God's glorious sons and daughters!" Let's learn these lessons and stand up in our destinies to demonstrate the glory and majesty of Jesus.

Contents

Thank you

I want to say a big thank you to my husband, Rick. His encouragement in my writing always presses me forward. I also appreciate him for reading through the manuscript to make sure my words matched my heart. Thanks for the edits, hun! We make a great team!

I also want to thank Father God for creating in me the creativity to write and giving me eyes to see beyond the natural. This is all from above, well the good parts are. Father Holy Spirit, thank you for the inspiration and bothering me with the stream of ideas. Jesus, thank you for making this entire relationship possible and granting me access to the throne room.

Introduction

One of my favorite movies of all time is "Signs." It is an M. Knight Shyamalan movie with Mel Gibson and Joaquin Phoenix. The main character, who was a pastor, has lost his wife to a car accident and is having difficulty trusting in God again. His brother has moved in with him to help raise the kids and to find a new normal. Before they can find that new normal, there is a global threat of an alien invasion. The main character is so angry with God that he refuses to see the signs that God has given him to make it through. He struggles with his beliefs as the threat becomes more personal.

You can watch this movie through the entertainment lens and get caught up in the aliens and/or see the signs' more profound meaning. This movie has been my favorite because of the signs and the hidden meaning that is written into the script.

Like the movie "Signs," you can see COVID-19 for face value and think, 'wow, she wrote a book that is going to have a limited shelf life.' Or you can view this current threat as just another threat to our humanity. It is vital to get our focus off the problem and look at how we respond to challenges. Step Out of Fear and Into Faith will help you see the signs of the Kingdom of God even in the language. It will show you how to have a Kingdom perspective and how God can use it. The lessons we learn from this threat will be the same whether we experience something together globally or if you have something that is personally impacting our life, such as a loss of a family member or a terminal diagnosis.

My hope in writing this book is to take the current threat of the day, since we are all in the same boat, and demonstrate Kingdom perspectives. This is an excellent opportunity because we are all in the same boat and can start at a common point. My intent is to make us stronger for the next storm by strengthening your relationship with the Father and His Kingdom.

Each chapter in this book is broken down into four sections;

current day observation, timeless truth, Kingdom perspective, and lessons learned. If this book manages to live past memory of the COVID-19 threat, then I hope you read it as a roadmap to step out of fear and into faith.

1. Contagious

Fear is Contagious

2020 Observation

"**Coronavirus disease 2019** (**COVID-19**) is an infectious disease caused by severe acute respiratory syndrome coronavirus 2 (SARS-CoV-2). The disease was first identified in December 2019 in Wuhan, the capital of China's Hubei province, and has since spread globally, resulting in the ongoing 2019–20 coronavirus pandemic."[1]

COVID-19 is very contagious. At first, the leaders feared the spread of COVID-19 to uncontrollable numbers and would overwhelm our healthcare systems. It was unknown how many lives would be taken by the virus. The estimated numbers were higher than what actually occurred. There were many fears surrounding COVID-19. Fear of overwhelming healthcare systems to masses of people dying from COVID-19. There was also the fear of the majority of the population getting COVID-19. COVID-19 pandemic created dangerous levels of paranoia that made everyone afraid of each other. The actual threat of the disease became secondary to the danger of fear COVID-19 produced.

---

1. https://en.wikipedia.org/wiki/
Coronavirus_disease_2019

Timeless Truth

Whether threatened or actual, storms of life will always produce fear for those who have their eyes set on the things in this world. The COVID-19 pandemic put the world in the same boat, well at least the same storm. It was something we experienced together, which made this particular threat unique. In all likelihood, we will probably not experience this again. However, fear is fear, whether felt independently as an individual or corporately.

When circumstances present themselves that threaten the way we live and force us to think about the future differently with unknown variables, it produces fear. When we submit to fear or give it undue attention, it becomes contagious. Fear impacts our lives in many ways. When our lives are threatened, and we are faced with a choice. Do we allow ourselves to be paralyzed by fear, or do we step out of fear and into faith? Faith is the antidote to fear.

Kingdom Perspective

The COVID-19 virus is contagious, but what was so surprising was the rapid spread of fear that overcame the world. We have watched the end-time movies, we have heard the last days preaching, and now we were faced with what could be an apocalyptic event. Whether you had the virus or not, we were all impacted by fear. Even if you have fear repellent and put your trust in the Lord at all times, you were affected by fear. Your job may have looked different, the way you shopped looked different, the way we could worship was different, and how we related to one another was different. Fear impacted us all!

According to Dictionary.com, "fear is a distressing emotion aroused by impending danger, evil, pain, etc., whether the threat is real or imagined." [2] Did you notice that, whether the threat is real or imagined? How many things are we afraid of that aren't real or aren't relevant to us?

There is a virus called COVID-19. It is contagious. There is a chance that you could contract the disease. There is a minimal chance that you will die from it. Granted, in March of 2020, we did not know what we know two months later. However, there were a lot of decisions made in fear and not on actual fact. So you have to ask yourself what is more dangerous to society, a real threat or imagined threat?

Whenever I hear the word fear or even feel fear, I also hear a response, "Fear not!" Father-God is often saying to His people to fear not. He must know something about fear because he says it a lot. Whenever God would visit people, He would say 'fear not.' It was often the first thing the Father spoke. We can't hear clearly until our fear is taken care of. When Father-God gave instruction to the heroes of the Bible regarding who they would become or the task that was in front of them, He said fear not first.

Look at Jesus' response to the disciples in Matthew 14. This is the story of Jesus walking on water and Peter wanting to join Him. Many of us know it well, but it is worth another look. Jesus and His disciples have just finished feeding the five thousand. He has instructed His disciples to head to the other side of the lake. Jesus was staying back to dismiss the people and spend some time in prayer to the Father.

The disciples find themselves in the middle of the lake amid high winds and heavy seas, being tossed about. Doesn't this feel like when we are in the middle of life's storms? We find ourselves in the middle of the storm being thrown to and fro with no sign of a Savior. But then Jesus comes walking on the waves. This is so amazing to think about. We often just recall this story as Jesus walking on water, He is walking on the waves! Look where the waves are? Where does Jesus

2. https://www.dictionary.com/browse/fear

put the storms of life? Under His feet. One lesson we can take from this is the storms of life are under the feet of Jesus.

The disciples are a little freaked out when they see Jesus. They think they see a ghost. It must not look like Jesus, or it is too dark to see Him clearly. Jesus puts their mind at ease immediately. Just like Father-God did with the people in the Old Testament. He tells them to not be afraid.

Jesus says in verse 27, "Be brave and don't be afraid. I am here!"

Jesus is saying that today as well. Don't be afraid of what you see happening. If we are in a relationship with Jesus, then Jesus is here. And Jesus puts life's struggles under His feet. Everything will bow at the name of Jesus.

You really have to love Peter. He is always first to want to step out and test the waters. Peter calls to Jesus and says if it is really you, have me join you. What does Jesus do? He says, come and join me. How did Peter know that it was really Jesus? The disciples mentioned in the earlier verse that they thought it was a ghost. Could the ghost not have called Peter out on the water? The important thing for us to know is that Peter couldn't tell in the dark of night and high winds if it was Jesus for sure. But Peter knew he didn't want to miss the opportunity if it was Jesus. He was willing to risk it. His faith in Jesus allowed him to step out. Many situations come our way, and we don't know for sure where Jesus is.

Back to our story, why just, Peter? There were twelve disciples, and only one of them stepped out? There was something special about Peter that he was more of a risk-taker. In the gospels, you will see Peter stepping up first to respond. Maybe it was the way Jesus introduced himself through the fantastic miracle of catching so many fish. Peter was usually the one who stepped out first, he also made mistakes and was corrected more. There is definitely a risk associated with stepping out in faith, but there is a great reward.

Back to the story, Peter stepped out and began to walk on water. He was doing it! But something overcame him. Peter became aware of the waves under his feet. The waves frightened him, and he began to sink. Where did Peter go wrong? Peter allowed the storms of life to be greater than the word of Jesus. He lost his focus and gave his attention to the problem instead of the promise.

The story doesn't end with Peter's sinking. Peter cries out for the Lord to save him. Jesus stretches out his hand and lifts Peter up. I think Jesus was disappointed at that moment. Not disappointed in Peter, but that doubt won and faith lost. Imagine the great time they would have had on the water if Peter was able to keep his eyes on Jesus. The rest of the disciples probably would have followed. It would have been a fantastic celebration and time of worship.

But worship still won out. When Jesus and Peter were in the boat, the disciples had a deeper understanding of who Jesus was, and they worshipped Him. Also, at that moment, the disciples had to realize Jesus wanted them to participate in these miracles as well. He invited Peter out of fear and into faith. Jesus wants us to recognize in Him we are above the storms of life. With our eyes fixed on Jesus, we can put all wind, waves, and storms under our feet. Giving in to fear will cause us to sink below what God has for us. Fear also has lots of company, there was a boat full of fearful disciples, except one brave disciple willing to step out of the boat of fear and into faith. Fear is contagious, but so is joy, love, and faith.

> 22 "As soon as the people were fed, Jesus told his disciples to get into their boat and to go to the other side of the lake while he stayed behind to dismiss the people.
> 23 After the crowds dispersed, Jesus went up into the hills to pray. And as night fell he was there praying alone with God.
>
> 24 But the disciples, who were now in the middle of the

lake, ran into trouble, for their boat was tossed about by the high winds and heavy seas.

25 At about four o'clock in the morning, Jesus came to them, walking on the waves! 26 When the disciples saw him walking on top of the water, they were terrified and screamed, "A ghost!"

27 Then Jesus said, "Be brave and don't be afraid. I am here!"

28 Peter shouted out, "Lord, if it's really you, then have me join you on the water!"

29 "Come and join me," Jesus replied.

So Peter stepped out onto the water and began to walk toward Jesus. 30 But when he realized how high the waves were, he became frightened and started to sink. "Save me, Lord!" he cried out.

31 Jesus immediately stretched out his hand and lifted him up and said, "What little faith you have! Why would you let doubt win?"

32 And the very moment they both stepped into the boat, the raging wind ceased. 33 Then all the disciples crouched down before him and worshiped Jesus. They said in adoration, "You are truly the Son of God!"

34 After they crossed over and landed at Gennesaret, 35 the people living there quickly recognized who he was. They were quick to spread the news throughout the surrounding region that Jesus had come to them. 36 So they brought him all their sick, begging him to let them touch the fringe of his robe. And everyone who touched it was instantly healed!" Matthew 14:22-36

"Be brave and do not be afraid! Jesus is here." Matthew 14:27

"Do not yield to fear, for I am always near. Never turn your gaze from me, for I am your *faithful* God. I will infuse you with my strength and help you in every situation. I will hold you firmly with my victorious right hand.'" Psalm 41:10

2. Wash Your Hands

Wash Your Hands of Earthly Perspectives

2020 Observation

During COVID-19, the Center for Disease Control put out this instruction for washing our hands:

- Wash your hands often with soap and water for at least 20 seconds, especially after you have been in a public place, or after blowing your nose, coughing, or sneezing.
- If soap and water are not readily available, use a hand sanitizer that contains at least 60% alcohol. Cover all surfaces of your hands and rub them together until they feel dry.
- Avoid touching your eyes, nose, and mouth with unwashed hands. [1]

Timeless Truth

No matter what point of history you experience, the world will try and seduce you into embracing the perspective of the day that is usually grounded in fear.

---

1. https://www.cdc.gov/coronavirus/2019-ncov/prevent-getting-sick/prevention.html

Kingdom Perspective

During the COVID-19 pandemic, we were told to wash our hands; we were taught how to wash our hands, when to wash our hands, and what to use when washing our hands. I thought it was interesting that the world was suddenly being trained on how to wash their hands. I had been doing it for years and was pretty good at it. Growing up, I remember I only washed my hands before I ate or if they felt dirty. Growing up as a kid who was outdoors a lot, I didn't notice my hands being dirty or didn't think about it. As I grew up and became a mother, I was aware of dirty hands all over everything. I became obsessed with washing my kiddo's hands. I could see their snacks on every toy, doorknob, shirt, stair rail, and the walls they touched. I became great at seeing the unseen and the microscopic. My clean, orderly, German roots kicked into high gear.

However, when I hear the words' wash your hands,' I don't think of getting rid of germs. Actually, my mind goes to the trial of Jesus. Pilate washed his hands during the trial of Jesus. Do you know this account or have you thought about the significance of it? The account is in Matthew 27:15-25 and is pretty powerful.

> *15 Now, every year at Passover it was the custom of the governor to pardon a prisoner and release him to the people—anyone they wanted. 16 And at that time, Pilate was holding in custody a notorious criminal named Jesus Barabbas. 17 So as the crowds of people assembled outside of Pilate's residence, he went out and offered them a choice. He asked them, "Who would you want me to release to you today, Jesus who is called Barabbas, or Jesus who is called the Anointed One?" 18 (Now, Pilate was fully*

aware that the religious leaders had handed Jesus over to him because of their bitter jealousy.)

19 Just then, as Pilate was presiding over the tribunal, his wife sent him an urgent message: "Don't harm that holy man, for I suffered a horrible nightmare last night about him!"

20 Meanwhile, the chief priest and the religious leaders were inciting the crowd to ask for Barabbas to be freed and to have Jesus killed. 21 So Pilate asked them again, "Which of the two men would you like me to release for you?"

They shouted, "Barabbas."

22 Pilate asked them, "Then what would you have me to do with Jesus who is called the Anointed One?"

They all shouted back, "Crucify him!"

23 "Why?" Pilate asked. "What has he done wrong?"

But they kept shouting out, "Crucify him!"

24 When Pilate realized that a riot was about to break out and that it was useless to try to reason with the crowd, he sent for a basin of water. After washing his hands in front of the people, he said, "I am innocent of the blood of this righteous man. The responsibility for his death is now yours!"

25 And the crowd replied, "Let his blood be on us and on our children!" Matthew 27:19-25

What lesson can come from this story that is relevant for today?

Pilate washed his hands because he didn't want to be associated with Jesus' death, and Pilate proclaimed his innocence in front of the crowd. This has far-reaching implications for the Jewish people and the judgment they would come under; however, that isn't what I am talking about.

Just as Pilate washed his hands from the guilt of Jesus' judgment, we need a ceremonial washing of our hands of earthly perspectives. This may be a stretch in your thinking, but to wash your hands of something means you no longer are part of it. We aren't called to disassociate ourselves from what is happening around us, but we are not part of it either.

> 19 *"If you were to give your allegiance to the world, they would love and welcome you as one of their own. But because you won't align yourself with the values of this world, they will hate you. I have chosen you and taken you out of the world to be mine."* John 15:19

We need to be reminded that we are a Kingdom people and not an earthly people. We are ambassadors of Heaven to this world, and we cannot get wrapped up in a worldly perspective and lose our Kingdom edge.

Pilate did not want Jesus' blood on his hands because it wasn't his fight. This pandemic, whether you believe it was for our health benefits or a power-play between liberals and conservatives, we cannot get caught up in the arguments of this world. If we do, we lose our Kingdom vantage point. We start fighting for victory instead of from victory; the victory and freedom already exist because we live by the spirit. We become part of the crowd or problem instead of the breakthrough that is so badly needed.

Let me share what it means to be living in the Kingdom of God. In the beginning, yes, we are going all the way back to the beginning. This isn't a new concept. In the beginning, God created the world.

He created man and woman in his image and gave them the authority to have dominion over every living thing. It was his Kingdom set up on earth to be ruled and reined over by his creation. That's us or Adam and Eve at the time. (summation of Genesis 1:26 by author)

In Genesis 3, Adam and Eve were deceived by the serpent and handed their God-given authority over to the enemy, Satan. He became the power of the prince over this earth, and the Kingdom of Darkness entered the world. Out of that sin, a curse was placed on man and woman, but a Savior, Jesus, was also promised. God considered those who came between Adam and Jesus righteous if they believed in Him and the promise of the Messiah.

When Jesus entered this earth as a baby, the Kingdom of God had come to earth. Jesus' entire ministry was to tell everyone the good news that the Kingdom of God was here. You can see the Kingdom of God breaking through when Jesus performed miracles, healings, or gave prophetic words. His death ended the Old Covenant that God had made with Moses to protect his people from the enemy and establish a new covenant that was much better. This covenant was between the Father and Jesus and could not be broken.

We are born sinners because of Adam's sin. But we are saved through Jesus' sacrifice and reconciled back to the Father. This was not just for the Jewish people but also for everyone who believes. When we accept Jesus into our hearts, the old man of Adam is buried, and we are raised as Jesus was as a new creation. This is excellent news. We are Kingdom people. The rules of the Kingdom are much different than those of this world. Jesus talked about it when He said things like:

- The last will be first.
- The weak will be strong.
- You serve to lead.
- You give to receive.

God's Kingdom economy is much different than this world. It is better. It changes the atmosphere, calms the storms, heals the sick, brings life to the dying, and grants peace to the restless.

We don't have a problem believing that when we die, things will be perfect. Life will be better. Our broken bodies will be healed. Our financial issues will be resolved. Our relational strife will be gone. We will be wise and free. What kingdom theology tells us, it is available now this side of Heaven. However, everything this side of Heaven will not be resolved because we still live in a fallen world. While the enemy has been beaten, he is still roaming the earth. He has been decommissioned but uses lies, intimidation, and fear to control and distract people from being reconciled to God. Sin is still prevalent, and the short and long-term impact still affects our lives. This in-between time of Jesus' resurrection and His second coming gives Jesus' followers, his bride, the church, the opportunity and authority to act on behalf of the Kingdom. We become ineffective because we do not understand this truth, and the enemy doesn't want us to get it.

In the context of Kingdom thinking, it is critical that we wash our hands of earthly perspectives and pick up the cross, not to bear the burdens, but to remember that the work Jesus did on the cross bought us access to the Kingdom, now. This is something that needs to be learned and relearned until it is part of your natural thinking. It will make a difference in how you live life as a new creation. Once you become proficient at this, you will see Kingdom in everything just as I saw dirt from my kids on everything. Instead of seeing kids hands-on, everything we will see God's hands-on everything.

We wash our hands of earthly perspectives and pick up the cross of Jesus, not just to bear one another burdens, but to remember that the work Jesus did on the cross bought us access to the Kingdom now.

"I have chosen you and taken you out of the world to be mine." John 15:19b

3. Vulnerable

You Are Able!

2020 Observation

There was a lot of talk about those who were vulnerable: over 65 years of age, obese, living in a nursing home, immunocompromised, diabetes, kidney and liver disease, serious heart and liver diseases. This group was labeled vulnerable for a higher risk of severe illness from COVID-19. There were degrees of impact for COVID-19 based on your level of vulnerability. The CDC classified the following as areas of vulnerability for higher risk of severe illness form COVID-19:

"Based on what we (CDC) know now, those at high-risk for severe illness from COVID-19 are:

- People 65 years and older
- People who live in a nursing home or long-term care facility

People of all ages with underlying medical conditions, particularly if not well controlled, including:

- People with chronic lung disease or moderate to severe asthma
- People who have serious heart conditions
- People who are immunocompromised
  - Many conditions can cause a person to be immunocompromised, including cancer treatment, smoking, bone marrow or organ transplantation, immune deficiencies, poorly controlled HIV or AIDS, and prolonged use of corticosteroids and other immune weakening

medications

- People with severe obesity (body mass index [BMI] of 40 or higher)
- People with diabetes
- People with chronic kidney disease undergoing dialysis
- People with liver disease"[1]

Timeless Truth

Being told that you are in a vulnerable class in never settling. It feels as if there is something you will be unable to do. The definition of vulnerable is open to attack or damage. Every threat exposes our vulnerability or weakness. When tested, we find our weakest point or breaking point. That point of knowing our vulnerability and being unable to mitigate the threat creates fear.

Kingdom Perspective

COVID-19 put us all in the same storm but not the same board. While the COVID-19 pandemic happened to all of us globally, it didn't uniformly impact us. Some felt threatened by the virus, some the economy, and some the long term impact on their rights. We all have different points of vulnerability. And we have an enemy that

1. https://www.cdc.gov/coronavirus/2019-ncov/need-extra-precautions/people-at-higher-risk.html

lives to exposes our vulnerability because it causes us to doubt God, sin, throws us into a panic, and creates havoc in our lives.

It is essential to know that we have a common enemy, Satan. Much of the world will blame God for a pandemic or any bad thing in our lives. Let's settle this once and for all, God is good, all the time! God can and will use this pandemic to further advance the Kingdom on Earth and our own lives, but He doesn't create the problem. But John 10:10 tells us the thief or Satan has the only destruction in mind, where God has only abundance and fullness is mind:

> *10 A thief has only one thing in mind—he wants to steal, slaughter, and destroy. But I have come to give you everything in abundance, more than you expect—life in its fullness until you overflow!"* John 10:10

This pandemic season is as if all those weak spots or points of vulnerability are exposed. Which gives the enemy the advantage to tempt and test us. Some believe the enemy is so clever to test our weaknesses. However, I don't believe the enemy is that powerful. The enemy has two tactics in his arsenal; fear and intimidation. What makes him look more clever than he is is how we respond to these two weapons. Our vulnerability shines where we are threatened. This pandemic proves that, same threat, different responses. Satan uses fear to intimidate us, God flips it and uses it to expose our level of strength and the area of our next upgrade.

We are in good company when we are tested. Jesus was tested at the beginning of His ministry, as told in Matthew 4. Satan tried to expose Jesus' vulnerability after spending forty days and nights fasting in the wilderness. Studying how Jesus' temptation will give us insight into how the enemy will work to expose our vulnerability. Setting the stage for Jesus' temptation is vital to understand the richness of this passage. Catch the first three verses of this passage

in Matthew 4. It is interesting. Look at the roles of the characters
and the backdrop of our story.

> "Afterward, the Holy Spirit led Jesus into the lonely
> wilderness in order to reveal his strength against the
> accuser by going through the ordeal of testing. ² And after
> fasting for forty days, Jesus was extremely weak and
> famished. ³ Then the tempter came to entice him to
> provide food by doing a miracle. So he said to Jesus, "How
> can you possibly be the Son of God and go hungry? Just
> order these stones to be turned into loaves of bread."
>
> ⁴ He answered, "The Scriptures say:
>
> Bread alone will not satisfy,
> but true life is found in every word,
> which constantly goes forth from God's mouth."
>
> ⁵ Then the accuser transported Jesus to the holy city of
> Jerusalem and perched him at the highest point of the
> temple ⁶ and said to him, "If you're really God's Son, jump,
> and the angels will catch you. For it is written in the
> Scriptures:
>
> He will command his angels to protect you
> and they will lift you up
> so that you won't even bruise your foot on a rock."
>
> ⁷ Once again Jesus said to him, "The Scriptures say:
>
> You must never put the Lord your God to a test."
>
> ⁸ And the third time the accuser lifted Jesus up into a
> very high mountain range and showed him all the

kingdoms of the world and all the splendor that goes with it.

⁹ "All of these kingdoms I will give to you," the accuser said, "if only you will kneel down before me and worship me."

¹⁰ But Jesus said, "Go away, enemy! For the Scriptures say:

Kneel before the Lord your God
and worship only him."

¹¹ At once the accuser left him, and angels suddenly gathered around Jesus to minister to his needs."

Matthew 4:1-11

Holy Spirit was leading Jesus to reveal his strength. Jesus was extremely weak and famished. The accuser, Satan, was there to test Jesus. The wilderness was even characterized as lonely. This sets our stage for the drama of our life. Holy Spirit is doing the leading, Satan is doing the testing, and the world is lonely.

Satan tries to tempt Jesus in three areas of potential vulnerability, they are ours as well: provision, identity and destiny, and inheritance. Jesus shows us how to respond and to find the upgrade that God desires to give us by living in a relationship with the Father, obeying God's voice, and worshipping God. Let me show you more clearly what I mean by breaking this passage into Satan's three attempts.

First attempt:

The accuser asks Jesus a question to try and entice Him. *"How can you possibly be the Son of God and go hungry? Just order these stones to be turned into loaves of bread."* In this question, He is pairing Jesus' identity with the fact that He is extremely hungry. The first part of the question is designed to raise doubt, the second part of the question is a lie. Someone less than Jesus may fall because they have to prove their identity by showing they can turn stones into bread.

Look at how Jesus responds to the attack on His identity and provision, *Bread alone will not satisfy,*

but true life is found in every word, which constantly goes forth from God's mouth." There are a couple of lessons in this statement. Jesus is going to use scripture to fight off the enemy, but also look at what He is saying, *"true life is found in every word, which constantly goes forth from God's mouth."* In order, to be safe from our vulnerabilities we have to be in a relationship with God, not just a Bible scholar.

Second attempt:

The enemy has learned some of Jesus' tactics of using Scripture, plus the accuser ups the anty by transporting Jesus to a high place to show Him all he has to offer. The accuser says,

"If you're really God's Son, jump, and the angels will catch you. For it is written in the Scriptures: He will command his angels to protect you and they will lift you up so that you won't even bruise your foot on a rock."

Clearly, the enemy has read some scripture and also understands God's promise to crush the enemy's head and bruise the foot of Jesus. He is now appealing to Jesus' destiny and mission on earth. He is tempting Jesus to be rescued by heaven and give up His mission. If you don't know the back story. When Adam and Eve sinned in the garden, they gave their authority and their offspring's authority to rule and reign over to the enemy. God cursed the serpent and told him that Eve's seed, Jesus, would crush his head and would bruise His heel. God promised a Savior that would be crucified and put an end to Satan's rule and reign over the world. Now Satan is tempting Jesus to bypass the pain and suffering of the cross.

Jesus responds by saying, *"The Scriptures say: You must never put the Lord your God to a test."* I struggled with this verse for a few minutes because we are told to test God with our finances in

Malachi. This verse says, "never." Jesus is quoting Deuteronomy 6:16. Here is what Malachi 3:10 says,

10 *"Bring all the tithes into the storehouse so there will be enough food in my Temple. If you do," says the Lord of Heaven's Armies, 'I will open the windows of heaven for you. I will pour out a blessing so great you won't have enough room to take it in! Try it! Put me to the test!'"* Malachi 3:10 (NLT)

If you look at Deuteronomy 6:16-17 that Jesus is quoting, 16 *"You must not test the Lord your God as you did when you complained at Massah. 17 You must diligently obey the commands of the Lord your God—all the laws and decrees he has given you.."*

What's the difference? Jesus says to not test God, God says to test him. Do you see it? In Malachi, God says to test him; in Deuteronomy, the Israelites are testing God, and in Matthew, Satan is telling Jesus to test God. It seems like it is okay to test God when He tells you to. When it comes to tithing, we can test and see how good God is. This has less to do with testing God and more to do with listening to God and what He says. Deuteronomy gives us a clearer picture of diligently obeying the commands of God.

Third attempt:

The accuser has one more temptation. Again, the accuser shows Jesus all the splendor of the kingdoms of the world and everything that entails. Here is Satan's offer:

9 *"All of these kingdoms I will give to you," the accuser said, "if only you will kneel down before me and worship me."*

The accuser, Satan, is providing Jesus a shortcut of taking back the Kingdom of God. Jesus came to earth to defeat the enemy and death while returning the authority of the Kingdom back to God and His people. Satan is saying, you don't have to defeat me, I will give it all to you, just bow down and worship me. What a liar! You get the Kingdom, but again you surrender rule and reign.

Satan is tempting Jesus with a short cut to the Kingdom without the pain and suffering of the cross. This would have destroyed everything, but Jesus was vulnerable. Go back to the first verse, this temptation was to reveal Jesus' strength. The Holy Spirit led him into a forty-day fast into a lonely wilderness; it makes complete sense that while weak and famished, his inner strength was growing. He proved it through Satan testing. He was vulnerable in the flesh but strong in the Lord.

The enemy, Satan, has a way of exposing our vulnerability. It is a tactic of any fight or battle to hit your opponent where they are weakest. The enemy is familiar with battle tactics. He is relentless at exposing our vulnerabilities. There is a risk in believing that Satan knows us so well that he can inflict this level of havoc in our life because we don't want to give him more power than he has or deserves. He doesn't have to be that good at it. There is a natural flow of life circumstances that create a testing ground to expose our weaknesses. For example, if you lose a job, how do you react? If a relationship ends, how do you react? If you get sick or discover you may have a disease, how do you react? If a loved one gets hurt, how do you react?

If we break it down, we can understand more clearly how this works. As humans, we have basic needs, and when those needs are at risk, it causes stress and anxiety. There are simple broad strokes that can be taken in our lives to expose the things we most worry about. If you were concerned about our safety, then your weakness could be exposed to a terrorist attack. If you worry about financial security, then losing your job or the threat of your job in jeopardy would be cause for concern. If you were worried about your health, then a threat to your health would be disconcerting. If you worried about your family, then anything that threatened them would make you take pause. Sin is also an access point for the enemy that leaves us vulnerable. That will be discussed in a later chapter.

The promise and hope for us are at the end of this passage in verse 11, *At once the accuser left him, and angels suddenly gathered around Jesus to minister to his needs.*" James 4 tells us that if we stand up to the devil and resist him, he will turn away or flee. God will move closer and minister to every need we have. God isn't concerned about your vulnerabilities. He is interested in what is missing from your life that leaves you vulnerable to the enemy attack. He has an upgrade of overabundant blessings to give you. Don't let yourself stay vulnerable, because **You Are Able** when you call upon Him.

> ⁶ *But he continues to pour out more and more grace upon us. For it says, 'God resists you when you are proud but continually pours out grace when you are humble.'*
>
> ⁷ *So then, surrender to God. Stand up to the devil and resist him and he will turn and run away from you.* ⁸ *Move your heart closer and closer to God, and he will come even closer to you. But make sure you cleanse your life, you sinners, and keep your heart pure and stop doubting."* James 4:6-8

Lesson Learned

The enemy uses fear to expose our vulnerability and weakness. Father God uses our vulnerability to reveal His goodness and promises an upgrade to strengthen and make us more than able. We are victorious!

"Fear and intimidation is a trap that holds you back. But when you place your confidence in the Lord, you will be seated in a high place." Proverbs 29:25

4. Disease

Sin is a Disease Too

2020 Observation

"People with COVID-19 have had a wide range of symptoms reported – ranging from mild symptoms to severe illness. Symptoms may appear 2-14 days after exposure to the virus. People with these symptoms may have COVID-19: cough, shortness of breath or difficulty breathing, fever, chills, muscle pain, sore throat, and new loss of taste or smell. Other less common symptoms have been reported, including gastrointestinal symptoms like nausea, vomiting, or diarrhea." [1]https://www.cdc.gov/coronavirus/2019-ncov/symptoms-testing/symptoms.html

---

Timeless Truth

COVID-19 is a disease that has a 99% recovery rate, where only 1% of the vulnerable population were expected to die. Sin is also a disease, but the mortality rate of sin is 100% for those who are not in a relationship with Jesus. With Jesus, the disease of sin has a profound impact on our life and the destiny that God has planned for us.

"Sin is a seed that brings a harvest; you'll reap a heap of trouble with

1.

every seed you plant. for your investment in sins pays a full return—the full punishment you deserve!" Proverbs 22:8

Kingdom Perspective

Most of this book is dedicated to a virus that we have no control over, but we should also address the impact of sin on our lives. There is a fear factor that directly correlates to the sin in our life. But, sin is a little different from areas of worry or concern over a virus or circumstances out of our control.

Not long ago, I was watching the last tribute to Billy Graham. Truly one of the great Christian Generals and Man of Faith of our time. He was talking about sin. He kept saying that sin is a disease. A disease that impacts so many areas of our life. That had a profound impact on my thinking. It moved from being a finger shaking correction to something we have to fight against. We know how a disease can impact so many areas of our life, I'm not sure that we consider the deadly impact sin can have on our lives and of those around us.

This isn't to make us sin conscious, but it is more of an understanding of what sin does in our life. Having sin in your life creates access points for the enemy to impact other aspects of our life. Using adultery as an example, if you choose to have an extra-marital affair, you have made your marriage and family an access point for the enemy. When you lie, then the enemy can use that lie to bring about anxiety if the truth comes out. Anything you are tempted to do that falls outside Kingdom living created an access point for the enemy to use in the future. At the very least, he will use it for guilt and shame.

Personally, I have experienced divorce in my life. This was something that I set in motion for many reasons. I don't know that I believe that divorce is a sin, but I do understand, first-hand, why God hates it. Separation creates multiple points of entry for the enemy. That's not to say the way we live in marriage may not also. Divorce is tearing apart, something that was designed to stay together. It doesn't come apart like pieces in a puzzle, but it more like those super glue commercials. Do you remember them? Two boards were super-glued together, and the only way they came apart was to tear up the wood. The glue was not meant to be released. So it breaks in different places. This is precisely what happens with divorce. Like the boards, it seems like they should neatly separate, but it damages both pieces of wood. One part of the wood has missing pieces, and the other plank has remnants of the other one. This is so true for divorce; one side is left feeling like they are missing something, and the other hand feels like they can't shake the splinters of the other spouse.

This one act of divorce creates splinters in all areas of our lives, friends, family, children, and our work. Our pasts are splintered, and our futures are no longer clear. The enemy loves divorce because he has so many access points for pain, heartache, financial ruin, harsh feelings, and can even impact generations with chronic problems. Divorce and the impact on our lives could be an entirely different book that I may tackle someday.

Even the best of us sin. King David experienced this, as well. He had an incredible relationship with God. He was known as the man after God's own heart. He experienced how one sin spread to many sins. Pretty soon, it had impacted his house for generations. Our story begins in 2 Samuel 11.

It started with King David deciding not to go off to battle even though all the other kings typically go out to war. We don't really know why he didn't go, but a great warrior that he was, there is some question. There is significance when David didn't go to war. The ark of the covenant went with the Israelites into battle. The ark of the covenant represented the presence of God. It seems David might be having a weak moment to let the ark leave without him.

After the warriors leave, David gets out of bed in the afternoon and sees Bathsheba bathing. He sends for her and sleeps with her. Bathsheba discovered she was pregnant and sent word to David.

King David wanted to cover up his discretion by sending for Bathsheba's husband, Uriah, so he could sleep with this wife. Uriah was considered one of David's mighty men. When David got the report of the war and sent Uriah home to sleep with his wife, Uriah went to sleep at the palace entrance. David asked why he didn't go home. Uriah's response, found in 2 Samuel 11: was one of honor and nobility, *"The Ark and the armies of Israel and Judah are living in tents, and Joab and my master's men are camping in the open fields. How could I go home to wine and dine and sleep with my wife? I swear that I would never do such a thing."*

David tried one more thing, he invited Uriah to dinner, got him drunk. He still did not go home to his wife and slept at the palace entrance again. David resorted to plan C of the great sin cover-up, murder. David sent Uriah back with a note for Joab telling him to station Uriah on the front lines where the battle is fiercest. Then pull back so that he will be killed. So Joab assigned Uriah to a spot close to the city wall where he knew the enemy's strongest men were fighting. And when the enemy soldiers came out of the city to fight, Uriah, the Hittite, was killed along with several other Israelite soldiers.

Bathsheba mourned for her husband. David sent for Bathsheba and made him one of his wives. Bathsheba gave birth to a son, and God was displeased with what David had done. The Lord instructed Nathan the prophet to go to David and tell him a story that made him come to realize he was the guilty one in all of this. In 2 Samuel 12:7-12, you find God's response to David.

> *7 Then Nathan said to David, "You are that man!*
> *The Lord, the God of Israel, says: I anointed you king of*
> *Israel and saved you from the power of Saul. 8 I gave you*
> *your master's house and his wives and the kingdoms of*
> *Israel and Judah. And if that had not been enough, I would*

> *have given you much, much more. 9 Why, then, have you*
> *despised the word of the Lord and done this horrible deed?*
> *For you have murdered Uriah the Hittite with the sword*
> *of the Ammonites and stolen his wife. 10 From this time*
> *on, your family will live by the sword because you have*
> *despised me by taking Uriah's wife to be your own.*
>
> *11 "This is what the Lord says: Because of what you have*
> *done, I will cause your own household to rebel against*
> *you. I will give your wives to another man before your*
> *very eyes, and he will go to bed with them in public*
> *view. 12 You did it secretly, but I will make this happen to*
> *you openly in the sight of all Israel."*

David took something that wasn't his. David had access to all of God's kingdom, and he chose to take something that wasn't his. He sinned, which led to more sins until it finally impacted Bathsheba, their son, and eventually, his household. David confessed his sin, but it was too late to save their child.

Bathsheba comforted David, and they had Solomon. The Lord loved this child, and all of David's favor was returned to Solomon's house. There were still remnants of sin in David's house, but God is a merciful and forgiving God.

Many think that when we sin, there really isn't a way back to God. And if there is, it isn't fully restored. Many times when we experience disease in the natural and recover from it, we say we are cancer survivors. We like to wear the battle, as a badge of courage. It is totally understandable, but God is a God of total healing. We need to leave our disease behind and fully embrace what Jesus did on the cross and look to see what God has next for us. We may be missing out on some awesome destiny. This is true for the disease of sin as well. Remember the cross, confess it, and move into guilt-free living. Embrace what God has next for you!

The old covenant provided a sacrificial lamb to forgive sins, but it never took care of the guilt and shame. Jesus's sacrifice takes care of sin and also guilt and shame, as well as the generational impact of our sin. We have to embrace the gift and live a life of freedom from the accuser. Put Jesus in the place of your sin and kick the disease to the curb once and for all.

Solomon, David's son, wrote about sin in Proverbs. He knew first hand the problem sin caused in the house of David as well as what he would experience later.

> *"Sin is a seed that brings a harvest; you'll reap a heap of trouble with every seed you plant. for your investment in sins pays a full return— the full punishment you deserve!"* Proverbs 22:8
>
> *"Arrogance, superiority, and pride are the fruits of wickedness*
> *and the true definition of sin."* Proverbs 21:4

I believe David's biggest misstep was when he didn't go to battle. It wasn't just because it exposed him to Bathsheba and temptation, but he allowed the spirit of God to go out of the palace without him. We should never get too far from the presence of God. The Holy Spirit is our guide to when we are heading into trouble. David knew that, as well. After David confessed and realized the gravity of his sins, David was most concerned about God's Spirit going away from him. Psalm 51 captures David's cry out for God's forgiveness. While it is easy to say, don't sin. The first step away from Father-God may be the one that leads to the biggest mistakes and heartbreak.

No matter what you have done, remember God is a God of second and third and fourth and multiple chances. The important thing is to come back to God. Father-God is waiting for you to turn back. In my experiences, He is always right behind me. I just wasn't aware. The journey back is closer than you think.

For the Pure and Shining One
A prayer of confession when the prophet Nathan exposed King David's adultery
with Bathsheba

1–2 God, give me mercy from your fountain of forgiveness!

I know your abundant love is enough to wash away my guilt.

Because your compassion is so great,
take away this shameful guilt of sin.
Forgive the full extent of my rebellious ways,
and erase this deep stain on my conscience.
3–4 For I'm so ashamed.
I feel such pain and anguish within me.
I can't get away from the sting of my sin against you, Lord!
Everything I did, I did right in front of you, for you saw it all.
Against you, and you above all, have I sinned.
Everything you say to me is infallibly true
and your judgment conquers me.
5 Lord, I have been a sinner from birth,
from the moment my mother conceived me.
6 I know that you delight to set your truth deep in my spirit.
So come into the hidden places of my heart
and teach me wisdom.
7 Purify my conscience! Make this leper clean again!
Wash me in your love until I am pure in heart.

[8] *Satisfy me in your sweetness, and my song of joy will
return.*

The places within me you have crushed
will rejoice in your healing touch.
[9] *Hide my sins from your face;*
erase all my guilt by your saving grace.
[10] *Create a new, clean heart within me.*
*Fill me with pure thoughts and holy desires, ready to
please you.*
[11] *May you never reject me!*
May you never take from me your sacred Spirit!
[12] *Let my passion for life be restored,*
tasting joy in every breakthrough you bring to me.
Hold me close to you with a willing spirit
that obeys whatever you say.
[13] *Then I can show to other guilty ones*
how loving and merciful you are.
They will find their way back home to you,
knowing that you will forgive them.
[14] *O God, my saving God,*
deliver me fully from every sin,
even the sin that brought bloodguilt.
Then my heart will once again be thrilled to sing
the passionate songs of joy and deliverance!
[15] *Lord God, unlock my heart, unlock my lips,*
and I will overcome with my joyous praise!
[16] *For the source of your pleasure is not in my
performance*
or the sacrifices I might offer to you.
[17] *The fountain of your pleasure is found*
in the sacrifice of my shattered heart before you.
You will not despise my tenderness

as I humbly bow down at your feet.
¹⁸ Because you favor Zion, do what is good for her.
Be the protecting wall around Jerusalem.
¹⁹ And when we are fully restored,
you will rejoice and take delight
in every offering of our lives
as we bring our sacrifices of righteousness before you in
love!
Psalm 51

Lesson Learned

Sin is a disease that has many symptoms and impacts many areas of our lives. It will limit our ability to step out in faith and threatens all that God has planned for us.

5. Self-Quarantine

Isolate the Fear

2020 Observation

During COVID-19, there was lots of talk about Quarantine and isolation. Initially, we were told or asked to self-quarantine for fourteen days to help stop the spread of the coronavirus. However, fourteen days turned in to a month, turned into two months, and then a little more. This was an historical request from the CDC and our governments. Most of the time, people who are sick are put in Quarantine, not healthy ones. You wouldn't necessarily believe that it could have a lasting impact on people, but remember anything you do for twenty-one days becomes a habit. People became fearful of stepping out because they were isolating themselves from an unseen virus and what others might have. Here is the request from the CDC:

Quarantine

"Quarantine is used to keep someone who might have been exposed to COVID-19 away from others. Quarantine helps prevent the spread of disease that can occur before a person knows they are sick or if they are infected with the virus without feeling symptoms. People in quarantine should stay home, separate themselves from others, monitor their health, and follow directions from their state or local health department.

Isolation

Isolation is used to separate people infected with the virus (those who are sick with COVID-19 and those with no symptoms) from people who are not infected. People who are in isolation should stay home until it's safe for them to be around others. In the home, anyone sick or infected should separate themselves from others by staying in a specific "sick room" or area and using a separate bathroom (if available)."[1]

Timeless Truth

Fear can impact many areas of our life. We can feel isolated in a crowd when we are fearful. Sometimes we believe we are the only ones experiencing fear. The enemy uses fear to create a feeling of isolation. Many times we self-quarantine because we are convinced others will not understand our fear.

Life seems very lonely, sometimes. Whether it is the hustle and bustle of people passing you by or being stuck in your home under quarantine orders, it just gets lonely. If you aren't experiencing loneliness, great! But we know by the suicide rate that many people feel alone with their problems, real or perceived. Millions of people suffer from depression. Being quarantined and isolated is a real issue when it comes to fear. The world responded to the fear of COVID-19 by quarantining, but at an individual level, we do the same thing. We run for cover when faced with fear. Sometimes, we would do anything rather than face it head-on.

Kingdom Perspective

You are never alone when you are in a relationship with Jesus.

1. https://www.cdc.gov/coronavirus/2019-ncov/if-you-are-sick/quarantine-isolation.html

Graham Cooke often says, "One person with God is always in the majority." [2] The Kingdom of God is all about flipping the worldview upside down. In this case, fear causes us to isolate ourselves, let's flip that and isolate the fear. Isolating the fear is about identifying it. Fear is a tricky emotion. It attaches to us and wants to become part of our identity. Maybe it's because when we were kids, we were called fraidy-cats if we were scared to do something. Are you a fraidy-cat, or are you a child of God who has a fear they need to isolate. When we can isolate the problem, then we can deal with it. We need to get good at naming our fears and bringing them to the Father in prayer.

Let's take a look at the Timai or Bar-Timeaus, depending on which translation of scripture you use. Timai's story is found in Mark 10. Jesus and his disciples are walking, and a large crowd joins them. Timai is a blind beggar. He hears of Jesus coming through and begins shouting out for him, "Jesus, son of David, have mercy on me now in my affliction. Heal me!"

The next part of this story is why we get stuck in our fears and problems. Verse 48 tells us the response of the crowd. They were indignant and scolded Timai for making such a racket. Doesn't that seem precisely what will happen to us if we share our problems? People will tell us to be quiet. Whether they are ignoring us, telling us others have it worse, giving advice that doesn't help, or some flip answer. All of these responses shut down a person in the middle of pain. The truth is, the crowd wants you to be quiet because they don't want to feel your problem. So we work hard at keeping all those fears shoved down inside where no one can see them. But the truth is, everyone can see them. The only one who is blind to your fears is you. Whoa!

2. Cooke, Graham. God's Keeping Power: Learning to Put Your Trust in God as Your 'Keeper'. BrilliantBookHouse, 2015.

Watch how Timai responds to the crowd. Wait, he didn't react to the crowd, he kept shouting for Jesus. This blind man is the bravest in the crowd. Jesus' response is always beautiful, "Call him to come to me." Jesus always wants to hear your problems first hand. It is calling you to bring your fear to him. Fight the crowd in your head that says not to say anything to be still and cry out to Jesus. Ignore them and press on to demand an audience with your Lord and Savior.

The disciples are big players in this scene as well. As the church and Christ-followers, the disciples are demonstrating our role pure and simple. We bring those in need to the feet of Jesus. We point them to the finished work of the cross. And we tell them to have courage, walk toward Jesus, He is calling for you. Isn't that beautiful. There it is! Have courage, walk toward Jesus, He is calling for you. Seriously, every verse of this passage is packed with symbolism and meaning. Timai throws off his beggar's cloak, jumped up, and made his way to Jesus. This beggars' cloak probably had pockets of money in it, and he leaves it behind. His excitement to get to Jesus should be our posture toward getting to Jesus. Timai thinks his life is going to change drastically, and he will no longer need his cloak. Let's face it, you can't have a real encounter with Jesus and remain the same. We need to ask ourselves, what are we holding on to that keeps us from getting close to Jesus.

This next part is the part that always confused me. Verse 51, Jesus asks him, "What do you want me to do for you?" Ummm, clearly, I'm blind. I want you to heal me. Nope, Timai doesn't skip a beat, "My Master, please, let me see again!" He is specific, and Jesus wants him to name his problem. Jesus wants to make sure you just don't want a better cloak or better corner. There is so much to learn from this. Jesus isn't going to heal your problem or your fear until you isolate the problem and identify it. The beggar wasn't probably just blind, he was perhaps displaced from his family, he was probably hungry, something on his body probably hurt, the only job he had was begging, etc. He needed to tell Jesus which problem He was running to Him with.

Jesus told Timai his faith had healed him. And Jesus restores his sight, the very thing he asked for. Timai demonstrates how our human conditions can make us feel isolated, but our faith is what heals us. Are we going to remain in our fear, or are we going to shout out for Jesus to come help? Don't let Jesus pass by or the crowd silence you (real or in your mind) and miss your chance to be healed. Jesus wants us to move towards faith, so He knows you believe Him for transformation.

But that isn't the end of the story. Timai began at once to follow Jesus. He didn't go back and pick up his cloak as far as we know. He followed Jesus. You see, when you experience the love and power of Jesus in such a magnificent way, it will evict you from your life. You won't be able to go back to what you were doing. When your fear is isolated, named, and Jesus heals you from it. You have to recreate your life. That can be a scary thing as well. But the one who healed you also has a plan for your life. This is your moment of truth. Are you going to step out of fear and into faith?

46 "When Jesus and his disciples had passed through Jericho, a large crowd joined them. Upon leaving the village, they met a blind beggar sitting on the side of the road named Timai, the son of Timai. 47 When he heard that Jesus from Nazareth was passing by, he began to shout "Jesus, son of David, have mercy on me now in my affliction. Heal me!"

48 Those in the crowd were indignant and scolded him for making so much of a disturbance, but he kept shouting with all his might, "Son of David, have mercy on me now and heal me!"

49 Jesus stopped and said, "Call him to come to me." So

Before leaving this topic, it is essential to see the results of self-quarantine and isolation with God. The absolute best story for this is the story of David and Goliath found in I Samuel 17. Before you read this portion of the story, it is important to understand David's back story. He was a young shepherd boy who was called a man after God's own heart. Their relationship was solid. David was the youngest of all his brothers and was anointed the future King of Israel at a young age. This did not sit well with his brothers or probably King Saul, who was reigning king.

Before David was King, King Saul and the Israelites were in a battle with the Philistines. The Philistines had this giant of a man that stood over nine feet tall. His name was Goliath. Goliath was taunting the Israelite army and offered to fight one man. Whoever wins, the others become their slaves. King Saul and the Israelites were shaken because this appeared to be a giant problem, pun intended. No one was willing to go out and fight the giant. This standoff went on for forty days.

David was sent by his father to the Israelite camp to bring some cheese sandwiches and check on his brothers. His brothers were none too happy that this little pip-squeak had shown up to report back to daddy. David left his shepherding and headed to the camp. David went to the camp and heard Goliath shout his taunt to Israel's army. The Israelite army ran away in fright. The men were saying, have you seen the giant? The King has offered a massive reward to anyone who kills him. He gets one of his daughters for a wife, and his family is exempt from paying taxes.

David wanted to be sure he heard the reward accurately, so he asked some other men. But David also identifies the fear. In 1 Samuel 17:26b, "Who is this pagan Philistine anyway, that he is allowed to defy the armies of the living God?"

This question that David asked comes from a relationship with the Father. He saw this pagan Philistine for who he was. Basically saying, who does he think he is? Don't you know my God is bigger? Remember: "One person with God is always in the majority." Plus, David knew God had a plan for his life. Well, David's question got back to King Saul. David told the King not to worry; he would fight this Philistine. Not only did David have faith in the fight, but he had been training on bears and lions, to protect his sheep. You probably know the rest of the story. David kills the giant with a slingshot.

This story differs from Timai's account because David had a relationship with the Father. Put these two stories together and understand how you can have faith over fear for yourself, and how you can do it for others. Timai changed his status in life, David changed an entire nation. He showed the army how to isolate the fear and charge in. This is the power we have in a relationship with the Father. David spent many days alone in the wilderness, chasing after God's heart. When we do the work in the relationship, we will come out swinging at giants and changing worlds.

Self-Quarantine with the Father and isolate fear.

"Have courage! Get up! Jesus is calling for you!" Mark 10:49b

[16] "We have come into an intimate experience with God's love, and we trust in the love he has for us. God is love! Those who are living in love are living in God, and God lives through them. [17] By living in God, love has been brought to its full expression in us so that we may fearlessly face the day of judgment, because all that Jesus now is, so are we in this world. [18] Love never brings fear, for fear is always related to punishment. But love's perfection drives the fear of punishment far from our hearts. Whoever walks constantly afraid of punishment has not reached love's perfection. [19] Our love for others is our grateful response to the love God first demonstrated to us." 1 John 4:16-19

This is a great footnote about Timai's name in The Passion Translation. "The footnote for Bar-Timaeus, son of Timaeus. "The name Timai is Aramaic and means "highly prized" (or "esteemed"). Though unable to see, he was highly prized in the eyes of Jesus, who stopped to heal him. The Greek transliteration is "Bar-Timaeus, son of Timaeus," which is somewhat confusing since the name Bar-Timaeus means "son of Timaeus." The Aramaic is to be preferred, for

Timai spoke Aramaic when he cried out to Jesus (v. 51), for "Rabbi" ("master-teacher") is an Aramaic title of respect."[3]

No matter your fears, position in life, or sicknesses, Jesus sees you as highly prized or esteemed. Remember, He went to the cross for you, that speaks volumes of your value to Him and the Kingdom of God. Never question how much you are loved by Jesus. He gave everything for you, you are "highly prized."

3. https://www.biblegateway.com/ passage/?search=Mark+10%3A46&version=TPT

6. Shelter in Place

God is my Shelter

2020 Observation

"Shelter-in-place is to seek safety within the building one already occupies, rather than to evacuate the area or seek a community emergency shelter. When the term shelter-in-place order was used by the authorities in the United States in responding to the outbreaks of Coronavirus disease 2019 (COVID-19) in 2020, people were not familiar with it as the term had been used in other emergency situations such as an active shooter which would require seeking a safe place to hide within the same building that the person already occupies until the situation is resolved. This caused confusion to the residents under the order on exactly what they were supposed to do. Later, the term stay-at-home order was used instead." [1]

Timeless Truth

No matter what is going on in our world, we always need a safe place. A place where we can hide from the storms of life, get away with our own thoughts, rest, and feel secure. Where is your safe place? Who, what or where is your shelter.

1. https://en.wikipedia.org/wiki/Shelter-in-place

Kingdom Perspective

*1 "God, you're such a safe and powerful place to find
refuge!*
You're a proven help in time of trouble—
*more than enough and always available whenever I
need you.*
2 So we will never fear
*even if every structure of support were to crumble
away.*
We will not fear even when the earthquakes and shakes,
moving mountains and casting them into the sea.
*3 For the raging roar of stormy winds and crashing
waves*
cannot erode our faith in you."   Psalm 46:1-3

It is easy to say, "put your confidence in God, and He will protect you from the storms of life" and much more difficult to do, especially when you are in the midst of the storm. For God to be an effective shelter, we need to understand His nature, build a relationship, test his promises, and never leave.

Our ability to see God as our shelter directly correlates with how we see God period. It is difficult to read scripture at face value and understand that God is loving. We see all the horrible things that happened to people in the Old Testament. The anger that would rise up. Many of us read our Bibles, looking at the characters of the Bible instead of God. We don't see how patient He is. We miss Him being inclusive to all nations. We see that He picks favorites. We don't understand how God could send His son to die for us. How cruel is that? However, this is more of the problem of the reader than of God. Our eyes do not see clearly the mystery and complexity of God.

The struggle is compounded by the people who follow Him. Many times it feels like it is a spectrum that ranges from judgmental to phony kindness. It can be very rare to find someone that is real and has a huge heart for God and people. As Christians, we have not lived out Kingdom principles well. We are a terrible sales team, promoting a hateful, vengeful God and a judgemental, phony people. Sign me up for that! I think not.

The good news is God is completely loving. This isn't a characteristic of His, it is who He is. God is love! He is completely safe. And He also has nothing but good thoughts about you. In fact, when we feel convicted of something. He isn't pointing the finger at your lack, He is showing you what you are missing and what He wants to give you. Usually, it is a deeper revelation of who He wants to be for you.

> *"The one who doesn't love has yet to know God, for God is love."* 1 John 4:8

The nature of God, which we may never fully understand this side of Heaven, is best understood inside the relationship. It is difficult to grasp Father-God as shelter if we only run to Him in times of trouble. A relationship allows us to understand His nature in every season. He has so much for us and wants to be with us. How do we build a relationship with the Father?

First, we need to have a relationship with Jesus. In John 14:6, Jesus explained, "I am the Way, I am the Truth, and I am the Life. No one comes next to the Father except through *union with me.* To know me is to know my Father too."

Second, every relationship requires time. When the relationship is new, time together allows you to get to know each other. A strong relationship requires you to spend more time together. As

Christians, we put more stock in what we do for God instead of spending time with Him. The story of Mary and Martha demonstrates this all too well in Luke 10. Martha was wrapped up in serving Jesus, while Mary wanted to sit at his feet and spend time with Him.

All of the great heroes of the Bible spent time with God: Jesus retreated to the mountains to spend time with God. Moses did, as well. Daniel spent time in worship to God. Esther spent time fasting and praying.

Third, we need to be honest with God. Elijah is such a great example of expressing himself to God in times of trouble. Things were looking pretty bad. Jezebel had massacred many prophets and had told Elijah the same was in store for him. Elijah ran to a safe place, and God's angels ministered to him. In 1 King 19:10, Elijah got up he told God, "I have been very zealous for the Lord God of hosts; for the children of Israel have forsaken Your covenant, torn down Your altars, and killed Your prophets with the sword. I alone am left, and they seek to take my life."

Elijah had a moment of awfulizing because he wasn't alone. It is great that we don't have to be completely honest and factual with God. He can handle our opinions, fears, and worries. Look at how God responds to him in verses 11 and 12, "'Go out and stand on the mountain before the Lord.'" And behold, the Lord passed by, and a great and strong wind tore into the mountains and broke the rocks in pieces before the Lord, *but* the Lord *was* not in the wind; and after the wind an earthquake, *but* the Lord *was* not in the earthquake; 12 and after the earthquake a fire, *but* the Lord *was* not in the fire and after the fire a still small voice."

God answered him with instructions for what to do next amidst this horrible event. He was sending 7,000 to help. This story is a great example of what looks like the end of the world, or at least the world we know when we bring it to God, He has a plan. But we have to know His voice. Father-God is not offended by our emotions.

One day God reminded me of a time with my teenage daughter, she was in a mood and would not talk to me. I kept bothering her to tell me until she blurted it out. It was a little dramatized and probably sounded as silly as she thought it would. But as a mom, I was so excited that she finally gave voice to it. I remember thinking; finally, I can deal with that. God let me know, this is exactly how he felt with me sometimes and Elijah. Blurting out the ridiculous gives God a place to start with our feelings. He helps us sort out fact from fiction from feelings. He gets us to a place of listening.

Finally, spending time with God allows us to recognize His voice and obey what He tells us. God told Elijah in I Kings 19 that God comes in a still small voice. Finding a quiet place to communion with God is beneficial to shut out the noise. It also helps us to hear Him when things aren't quiet, because we know Him and can get to that inner place quickly. There is an intimacy that begins to develop with God.

> ⁵ *"Trust in the Lord completely,*
> *and do not rely on your own opinions.*
> *With all your heart rely on him to guide you,*
> *and he will lead you in every decision you make.*
> ⁶ *Become intimate with him in whatever you do,*
> *and he will lead you wherever you go."*
>
> Proverbs 3:5-6

When we understand God's nature and develop a relationship, we can trust in the shelter of the Most High and never leave it. At least, never leave it long enough for the enemy to steal what God has deposited in our life. God's mercies are new every morning, and He longs to give us fresh words before we step out. Let's close this chapter with a word from King Solomon in Proverbs 8. And get to

the place where we will wait at wisdom's doorway to hear a word
every day.

> ^{32} "So listen, my sons and daughters, to everything I tell
> you,
> for nothing will bring you more joy than following my
> ways.
> ^{33} Listen to my counsel,
> for my instruction will enlighten you.
> You'll be wise not to ignore it.
> ^{34} If you wait at wisdom's doorway,
> longing to hear a word for every day,
> joy will break forth within you as you listen for what I'll
> say.
> ^{35} For the fountain of life pours into you every time that
> you find me,
> and this is the secret of growing in the delight
> and the favor of the Lord."
>
> Proverbs 8:32–35

Lesson Learned

"The size of faith is always a lesser issue than where it is placed."[2]

This quote from Graham Cooke is becoming one of my favorites. When we think of faith, we often think of the size of our faith and that it can move mountains. Rarely, if ever, is it addressed about what we put our faith in. The mountains can move from mustard seed-sized faith because that mustard seed has been placed in God's hands. It's not how great our faith is, it is how big our God is. God is our shelter in and out of trouble. Stepping out of fear and into what God has entirely depends on where your faith is being placed.

> *"But the one who always listens to me will live undisturbed in a heavenly peace. Free from fear, confident, and courageous, you will rest unafraid and sheltered from the storms of life." Proverbs 1:33*
>
> *"But in the day that I'm afraid, I lay all my fears before you and trust in you with all my heart." Psalm 56:3*

2. Cooke, G., 2015. The Language Of Promise. 1st ed. Vancouver, WA: Brilliant Book House, p.33.

7. Mask

Mask Your Eyes and Ears and Put on the Mind of Christ

2020 Observation

"The Center for Disease Control (CDC) continues to study the spread and effects of the novel coronavirus across the United States. We now know from recent studies that a significant portion of individuals with coronavirus lack symptoms ("asymptomatic") and that even those who eventually develop symptoms ("pre-symptomatic") can transmit the virus to others before showing symptoms. This means that the virus can spread between people interacting in close proximity–for example, speaking, coughing, or sneezing–even if those people are not exhibiting symptoms. In light of this new evidence, CDC recommends wearing cloth face coverings in public settings where other social distancing measures are difficult to maintain (e.g., grocery stores and pharmacies), especially in areas of significant community-based transmission."[1]

Timeless Truth

If fear is the contagion, then masking our face is inappropriate.

1. https://www.cdc.gov/coronavirus/2019-ncov/prevent-getting-sick/cloth-face-cover.html

Our minds are what is at risk of catching the disease. Instead of protecting our breathing, we need to protect what we hear and see. We need to mask our eyes and ears from worldly thinking.

Kingdom Perspective

> [1]Beloved friends, what should be our proper response to God's marvelous mercies? I encourage you to surrender yourselves to God to be his sacred, living sacrifices. And live in holiness, experiencing all that delights his heart. For this becomes your genuine expression of worship.
>
> [2] Stop imitating the ideals and opinions of the culture around you, but be inwardly transformed by the Holy Spirit through a total reformation of how you think. This will empower you to discern God's will as you live a beautiful life, satisfying and perfect in his eyes. Romans 12:1-2

In this season of a global pandemic, where the world is telling you what to think, how is your own critical thinking? What is critical thinking? Critical thinking is defined by the objective analysis and evaluation of an issue in order to form a judgment.

One of the areas I have been most surprised by is our inability to think critically. What I mean by that is that we have lost our minds! I don't say that because the world doesn't have the same views that I do, I say that because there has been very little evidence to demonstrate, we are thinking on our own. My conclusion is that everyone has lost their minds. Granted, that may be overstating it, but I can't help but think we have given away our ability to think.

We are living in a world where we hold tight to opinions, but I don't believe they are our own. Some may say we have lost our ability to honor the views of others. I wonder what came first, the chicken or the egg in this case. I have a hard time accepting your opinion because I don't think it is yours, I think it is an opinion you have borrowed from someone else.

Our mind is our own, the Father says in Romans 12:2 be transformed by the renewing of your mind. Or in The Passion Translation, it tells us this:

Stop imitating the ideals and opinions of the culture around you, but be inwardly transformed by the Holy Spirit through a total reformation of how you think. This will empower you to discern God's will as you live a beautiful life, satisfying and perfect in his eyes.

So why do we give this up so freely? If we have surrendered our lives to Christ and identify with Him as a son or daughter, why in Heaven would you give up your right to think critically and be informed by what the Holy Spirit is telling you?

There are a couple of reasons why we fall into this behavior and have relinquished our critical thinking ability.

1. We have a desire to belong to something bigger than ourselves. Sharing opinions and beliefs of others allow us to experience a sense of belonging. To think for yourself, or better yet, let Holy Spirit inform you, is a risk of stepping out of that comfort zone that the crowd affords you. It may require you to step into the oncoming fire of contrary opinions, which may alienate you from the crowd.
2. What if you are wrong? Our desire to be right is powerful. If we share an opinion that isn't shared, and then it turns out to be incorrect, we may experience shame and social distancing of a different kind. The risk seems too high.
3. We lack the energy for the fight. Sometimes it just seems like

there are fights that aren't worth fighting. When we go against
mainstream thinking, it takes energy to hold your ground,
whether you are outwardly sharing your thoughts or silently
holding your ground and refusing to buy into popular opinion.

How do we step out of fear and regain our ability to think critically
and, better yet, allow the Holy Spirit to inform our opinions and
beliefs?

Turn down the voice of the crowd.

It doesn't take long to get a sense of what the crowd is saying.
Turn on any news outlet or scroll through Facebook, and you will
uncover the opinion of the day. For us to think critically, we have
to be willing to shut down the noise. You may need to turn it off
entirely for a season, or you may be able to turn it down. What do I
mean by turning it down? Get to a place where you only watch and
read enough to understand the pulse of the crowd and then shut it
off to avoid being influenced by it.

Being able to share the crowd's opinion doesn't make you more
intelligent, it actually just proves that you can parrot what others
are saying. Rational and critical thinking comes from your ability
to formulate your own opinion that may have some similarities and
recognize where your thoughts move in a different direction.

Here is a little secret to the toxic crowd opinions. There is an
element of truth to the opinions being shared; however, they are
paired with lies, fear, and intimidation, which is an excellent recipe
for herding more people into the crowd. This is the enemy's tactic;
use a little bit of truth, so you cannot deny the opinion but pair it
with fear and lies to create higher levels of chaos. Brilliant? Yes, but
we are smarter.

Have a desire for more of the heart of the Father.

Our desire to understand the Father's heart should be greater
than our willingness to hear the worldly opinions that are going
on. The Father-God has a plan. His ways are great, and our desire
should be to have the mind of Christ. Look at the promise in
Colossians 2:7-9 (TPT) emphasis added:

> 7 "*Your spiritual roots go deeply into his life as you are continually infused with strength, encouraged in every way. For you are established in the faith you have absorbed and enriched by your devotion to him!*
>
> *8 Beware that no one distracts you or intimidates you in their attempt to lead you away from Christ's fullness by pretending to be full of wisdom when they're filled with endless arguments of human logic. For they operate with humanistic and clouded judgments based on the mindset of this world system, and not the anointed truths of the Anointed One.*
>
> *9 For he is the complete fullness of deity living in human form.*
>
> *10 And our own completeness is now found in him. We are completely filled with God as Christ's fullness overflows within us.* **He is the Head of every kingdom and authority in the universe!**" Colossian 2:7-9

Do you see that? He is the Head of every Kingdom and authority in the universe. It doesn't say except earth. We are part of that universe. Instead of letting the crowd inform your opinion, why wouldn't we want to seek the Father and His Kingdom? He is the Head, and the good news is He lives in us if we have received Him.

Train ourselves to have a Kingdom perspective on all of our situations.

Understanding the Kingdom of God is key to separating yourself from the fear and panic of this world. As Christians, we can see the Kingdom of Heaven breaking through into earth. Jesus told us to pray for God's Kingdom to come and be done on earth as it is in Heaven. When we understand the Kingdom, we understand that we live in a new reality or realm. As Christians, it is not in our nature to be part of the crowd, because it defies our Kingdom reality. The world sees disease, death, and fear, and as Kingdom ambassadors, we see the opportunities arising from what the enemy means for evil. But we have to train ourselves to put on our Kingdom lens or goggles. We exchange our worldview for a Kingdom-based worldview. It allows us to see hope, promise, opportunity, and abundance. Make no mistake, this isn't rose-colored glasses, it is a Kingdom reality of God's goodness breaking through. We set our minds on things from above.

> *"Yes, feast on all the treasures of the heavenly realm and fill your thoughts with heavenly realities, and not with the distractions of the natural realm."* Colossians 3:2

Pray for confidence, boldness, and opportunity to be the Kingdom representative in the crowd.

No doubt, it is difficult to have a differing opinion. However, it is our birthright to have the mind of Christ. It is our responsibility and privilege to represent the King Jesus and the Kingdom of God here on earth. We are all called to be leaders, and leaders have to buck the system and go against popular opinion. We have no hope of transforming this world if the church, you and me, stays silent. The enemy is counting on our fear, counting on you placing your comfort over your responsibility and counting on our tendency for mediocrity instead of a willingness to stand firm. But God believes in us and has much higher thoughts, He has equipped us with what we need to stand firm, given us armor because He knows we have been born into a battle. But we are His, and He is ours, and we are warriors. And we cannot fail.

[7] *For God will never give you the spirit of fear, but the Holy Spirit who gives you mighty power, love, and self-control.* 2 Timothy 1:7

[28] *So we are convinced that every detail of our lives is continually woven together to fit into God's perfect plan of bringing good into our lives, for we are his lovers who have been called to fulfill his designed purpose.* [29] *For he knew all about us before we were born and he destined us from the beginning to share the likeness of his Son. This means the Son is the oldest among a vast family of brothers and sisters who will become just like him.* Romans 8:28-29

Having the mind of Christ in every situation is a beautiful gift from God. Let's not waste what God has intended by being earthly minded. Use all that the Holy Spirit empowers you with to think critically and with the heart of the Father.

Lesson Learned

Putting on the mind of Christ is crucial to critically thinking.

8. Social Distancing

Holy Spirit Violates Social Distancing

2020 Observation

During COVID-19, social distancing was recommended to reduce the spread of the virus. "Social distancing, also called "physical distancing," means keeping space between yourself and other people outside of your home. To practice social or physical distancing: Stay at least 6 feet (about 2 arms' length) from other people, do not gather in groups, and stay out of crowded places and avoid mass gatherings."[1]

Timeless Truth

When we are struggling in difficult times, it is common for us to want to distance ourselves from others. How many times have you left or wanted to leave a room when things are difficult or heated. If you haven't, you all know those who have. Sometimes, we need to put space between the situation and ourselves as to not infect others. At times we just want to be alone because it is just too painful to be around others. We don't trust our feelings, or we aren't

1. https://www.cdc.gov/coronavirus/2019-ncov/prevent-getting-sick/social-distancing.html

sure people will understand. Many times we feel we have to distance ourselves from others until we figure it out.

Kingdom Perspective

We often have a tendency to withdraw from God, we don't trust Him with our problems, and we aren't sure He has our best in mind. Usually, when something is going wrong, we are replaying a parental instruction that tells us to figure it out, stop doing it, or just get over it. When our back is against the wall, it can be a matter of fight or flight. And we all have racked up many frequent flyer miles.

Distancing ourselves from situations is not a new thing. The story of Jonah is all about distancing from God. In Jonah 1:1, God is giving Jonah an assignment. Get up and go to the great city of Nineveh. Nineveh is an evil city that Jonah has probably experienced personal loss from their actions. Look at Jonah's response in verse 3. "Jonah got up and went in the opposite direction to get away from the Lord."

Jonah didn't wander off course, he didn't question God. Jonah put as much distance from God and His instruction as possible, he bought a ticket in the opposite direction.

> [1] *"The Lord gave this message to Jonah son of Amittai:*
> [2] *"Get up and go to the great city of Nineveh. Announce my judgment against it because I have seen how wicked its people are."*
>
> [3] *But Jonah got up and went in the opposite direction to*

God's response is found in verse 4: "But the Lord hurled a powerful wind over the sea, causing a violent storm that threatened to break the ship apart." The sailors were desperate, praying to their gods and casting lots to see which one had offended the gods. In the meantime, Jonah, our runner, was taking a nap. The sailors woke him. Jonah told him that he was the one that disobeyed his God. Jonah said, well, you can fix this; just throw me into the middle of the storm.

The reader has to capture that Jonah isn't worried about disobeying God, he can sleep through a storm that sailors fear, and he requests to be thrown into the middle of the storm. It is safe to say that Jonah is vehemently opposed to his mission. He would rather do anything than go to Nineveh. Ironically, in the middle of Jonah's disobedience, every sailor vowed to serve God. Because as soon as Jonah was in the water, the storm stopped.

Jonah was swallowed up by a big fish for three days. God put Jonah in a fishy time out and the ultimate social distancing. Jonah found the energy and will to pray. And finally, In Jonah 2:9, he circles back to his senses. "But I will offer sacrifices to you with songs of praise, and I will fulfill all my vows. For my salvation comes from the Lord alone." His timeout set him straight, and he is now willing to fulfill his vows as a prophet to Nineveh. The Lord ordered the fish to spit him out on the beach.

It doesn't matter how far we run from God, he will draw us back to him. It doesn't matter how distant we are from God or where the storms from God take us. He cannot help himself to draw close to us. His Spirit, the Holy Spirit, always draws close, even in the belly of a fish.

Again, God tells Jonah to go to Nineveh and deliver the message God had given to him. Nineveh obeyed. He went into the streets of Nineveh, smelling fishy and probably standing out a bit. But this time, Jonah obeyed. He shouted out, "Forty days from now Nineveh will be destroyed."

³ *"This time Jonah obeyed the Lord's command and went to Nineveh, a city so large that it took three days to see it all.* ⁴ *On the day Jonah entered the city, he shouted to the crowds: "Forty days from now Nineveh will be destroyed!"* ⁵ *The people of Nineveh believed God's message, and from the greatest to the least, they declared a fast and put on burlap to show their sorrow."* Jonah 3:3-5

A side note the forty-day thing keeps showing up. The people of Nineveh embraced the message, even the King of Nineveh, called for a change. The city turned from their evil ways, and God changed His mind about bringing down judgment on the city.

This would be a great end to our story of what God can do when we try to distance ourselves from God. How he violates our space on the regular to bring more people to him. But Jonah wasn't happy. Jonah just delivered the news that saved a large city from destruction, and Jonah is ticked. Our guy, Jonah, complained to God. He's learning, he didn't just run, that doesn't end well. But he is still complaining.

Jonah is having a full-on dramatic fit! Jonah says I knew you would do this. I knew you would be merciful and compassionate, so to anger filled with love. That's why I didn't want to come to Nineveh. Clearly, Jonah hated the Ninevites. Jonah tells God, "Just kill me now, I'd rather be dead." He gave him 'it's them or me, God.' And of course, you will choose them because you are so kind and loving.

If you don't think God is a God of self-control and patience, read the next verses. Because don't you just want to smack Jonah down. Jonah pulls another distancing move. And God is so good, He provides Jonah with some shade that gave Jonah comfort during his hissy fit. He also taught him a lesson about compassion.

> The sun beat down on his head until he grew faint and wished to die. "Death is certainly better than living like this!" he exclaimed.
>
> [9] Then God said to Jonah, "Is it right for you to be angry because the plant died?"
>
> "Yes," Jonah retorted, "even angry enough to die!"
>
> [10] Then the Lord said, "You feel sorry about the plant, though you did nothing to put it there. It came quickly and died quickly. [11] But Nineveh has more than 120,000 people living in spiritual darkness, not to mention all the animals. Shouldn't I feel sorry for such a great city?"

In this fish story, we often miss the nature of God. We are so busy looking at the fish or whale, discussing if it is possible and thinking about how Jonah could live like that, then we miss God in the story. When we distance ourselves from God, he doesn't just stand there and watch us go. He chases after us, He uses the Holy Spirit to speak to our inner being. God wants to use us to advance His Kingdom. God is so good, loving, and merciful that He is saving people in the midst of our disobedience and bad attitudes. First, the desperate sailors and then the great city of Nineveh.

Father-God, our Creator, wants to be close to all of His creation, He will go to great lengths.

Jesus left Heaven to invade our space, He returned to Heaven and gave us the great encourager, the Holy Spirit. And the Holy Spirit will always violate the social distancing parameters. Scripture tells us so. Whether you are excited or depressed. The Spirit of God is still with us. That should comfort us in every season, especially in those dark seasons of our life when we feel alone or when we feel like running.

Our relationship with the Holy Spirit is very important for how well we do Kingdom Life. The Holy Spirit was promised to us by

Jesus before he ascended into Heaven. The Father never intended for us to be alone, so He promised us the gift of the Holy Spirit. The Holy Spirit is a down payment for our heavenly inheritance.

Lesson Learned

Holy Spirit is our gift from God as an internal encourager who is never distant from us.

⁷ *"Where can I go from your Spirit?*
Where can I flee from your presence?
⁸ *If I go up to the heavens, you are there;*
if I make my bed in the depths, you are there."

Psalm 139:7–8

Reflect on these verses and always trust that you are never alone, God is with you!

Phil 2:1 *"Look at how much encouragement you've found in your relationship with the Anointed One! You are filled to overflowing with his comforting love. You have experienced a deepening friendship with the Holy Spirit and have felt his tender affection and mercy."*

John 15:26 *"And I will send you the Divine Encourager*[2] *from the*

2. [c]

very presence of my Father. He will come to you, the Spirit of Truth, emanating from the Father, and he will speak[3] *to you about me."*

John 16:15 "*Everything that belongs to the Father belongs to me—that's why I say that the Divine Encourager will receive what is mine and reveal it to you.*"

2 Cor 3:17 "*Now the Lord is the Spirit, and where the Spirit of the Lord is, there is freedom.*"

John 14:26 "*But the Advocate, the Holy Spirit, whom the Father will send in my name, will teach you all things and will remind you of everything I have said to you.*"

John 14:16 "*And I will ask the Father, and he will give you another advocate to help you and be with you forever.*"

3. [d]

9. T.P.

Totally Prosperous not Totally Paranoid

2020 Observation

When COVID-19 became a real threat and lockdown seemed imminent, the stores were flooded with last-minute preppers. We were doing regular shopping for a church event at one of the large box membership stores. The toilet paper aisle was completely empty. We headed over to a large grocery store, and they were gone as well. Even though a small amount of fear came over me, I wasn't that worried, but I was curious. We then headed to a large hardware store, gone!

Toilet paper was the hot commodity for COVID-19. The reasoning was it was a large item that took a lot of space at the stores. It was also an item that most stores do not keep on hand because of its volume. The toilet paper shortage created a secondary reaction. Seeing an aisle of empty shelves created a scarcity mentality that groceries would be hard to get. Thus creating this trickle-down effect or rush on grocery items.

Ironically, weeks later, there were reports of milk and eggs being thrown out because demand and distribution channels were not keeping up with supply. Also, during this time, a barrel of oil dropped to under a dollar. I'm not sure how that happens in the commodity world. It sounds like they had to pay for people to take it. The gas prices went from mid two dollar range to just over a dollar. Ironically, our scarcity mindset created an overabundance we didn't have access to in less than six weeks.

Timeless Truth

The concept of feast and famine is not a new one. Our fear is directly related to a perception of what we lack. If we lack provision, lack security, lack finances, or lack relationships, these all result in fear. Many anxious people have a fear of something. The worry that something will change, and it will be a detriment in their life. We start playing the what-if game. Do you notice when people play what-if, it is usually negative? "What if I can't get toilet paper? Then I should go buy all I can now."

I remember playing this game with my oldest son. When he was in first grade, he worried about missing the bus, so much so he would leave the house very early. The anxiety that he produced caused me a lot of concern. (Wow, fear is contagious.) I decided to play the "what-if" game.

I asked, "What if you miss the bus?"

He said, "I'd walk home."

I asked, "Then what would we do?"

He said, "You'd take me."

I asked, "Will you get there on time?"

He said, "No, I would be early."

I asked, "Then, if you know this, why are you worried?"

A couple of weeks into the pandemic, I thought that we hadn't had beef in a while. I didn't have any in the freezer, and I hadn't seen much in the meat cases. I decided to go to the grocery store, and on the way, I prayed for beef, eggs, and toilet paper. At that time, those three were the at-risk items. Each section that contained these three items were freshly re-stocked with a few options, even the toilet paper. I thanked God at that moment for how He had provided.

The core issue becomes our level of trust in God to provide for us in every season. How much do you trust Him? A global fear pandemic can definitely test your level of trust.

Kingdom Perspective

The Kingdom's perspective is that God always provides for us. He tells us in so many ways in scripture. In fact, He tells us that we will prosper. As Christians, we have been so confused about money, provision, and the Kingdom, with good reason. Somewhere in our minds, we have these things clouding our perception of provision:

- taking a vow of poverty
- difficult for a rich man to enter the Kingdom of Heaven
- money is the root of all evil
- the prosperity gospel is bad
- the T.V. evangelist promising health and wealth if we give an offering
- we are in debt because we are stupid
- Jesus turning over the tables of the money changers in the temple

With all of these thoughts, we have a tendency to just divorce our spiritual life from our financial one. It is much easier if I don't have to think about them together. The enemy has won if we do this. But the core issue isn't the perception we have of money; it is our perception of God's nature.

We think there is credibility to the vow of poverty because, for some reason, God wants us poor. We are needier that way. Or we have this crazy performance-based thinking that I need to give something in order to get something. Let me put your mind at ease right now. God doesn't need anything from us. He wants your love, but even that He will give us the love to give back to Him. Think of this like a parent giving their children money to go buy a birthday present for the mom or dad. The parents give the child money to include them in on the joy it is to give. God is the same way, He provides us with what He needs. There isn't anything we need to scrape together to give to God.

If we have a great sense of lack in our life, it's maybe because we have this performance wheel in our mind that we haven't done enough to deserve being taken care of. Now God has sent this virus or test to show that we have been bad humans, and He is ready to take us out. NOTHING could be further from the truth. The enemy is the one who tells us this. Satan's tactics always get us to work or pay for something that God has already provided.

Psalm 23:1 says, "the Lord is my shepherd, I shall not want." If we are feeling a sense of lack, it is because we don't know the Good Shepherd. God's very nature is to provide for His children. Our lack is more about our lack of understanding of the nature of God. It becomes an invitation to press in and understand who God wants to be for you.

Jesus is directly addressing this issue in the Sermon on the Mount. Read through this passage in Matthew 6 and look at the promises.

> 25 *"This is why I tell you to never be worried about your life, for all that you need will be provided, such as food, water, clothing—everything your body needs. Isn't there more to your life than a meal? Isn't your body more than clothing?*
>
> 26 *"Look at all the birds—do you think they worry about their existence? They don't plant or reap or store up food, yet your heavenly Father provides them each with food. Aren't you much more valuable to your Father than they?* 27 *So, which one of you by worrying could add anything to your life?*
>
> 28 *"And why would you worry about your clothing? Look at all the beautiful flowers of the field. They don't work or toil,* 29 *and yet not even Solomon in all his splendor was robed in beauty more than one of these!* 30 *So if God has clothed the meadow with hay, which is here for such a*

*short time and then dried up and burned, won't he
provide for you the clothes you need—even though you live
with such little faith?*

*³¹ "So then, forsake your worries! Why would you say,
'What will we eat?' or 'What will we drink?' or 'What will
we wear?' ³² For that is what the unbelievers chase after.
Doesn't your heavenly Father already know the things
your bodies require?*

*³³ "So above all, constantly chase after the realm of
God's kingdom and the righteousness that proceeds from
him. Then all these less important things will be given to
you abundantly. ³⁴ Refuse to worry about tomorrow, but
deal with each challenge that comes your way, one day at
a time. Tomorrow will take care of itself."*
Matthew 6:25-34

The promise is so incredible. Jesus isn't telling us we will be happy with the portion that He gives us and expect it to be small and insignificant. He is telling us that King Solomon, the richest man in the world to date, paled in comparison to the birds of the air and the flowers in the field. He has you covered. During this pandemic, this is an area that has stood out to me. Everything seems to be changing of what man has created, but what God has created hasn't changed. The sun comes up in the morning, the moon shines at night. The birds are still singing a lot, which seems to be one of our prettiest springs I can remember. I could be noticing it more because my busyness has subsided, but I think God is showing us that He never changes. That what He puts in place has lasting life.

The Father wants you to know, He's got you, he loves you! God is not a God of measure, He is a God of abundance. He can't help but multiply, it is His nature. Think about an apple. It holds seeds that contain future orchards. Even a woman, carrying a child, is also carrying her grandchild. Wow!

There is an instruction that Jesus gives at the end of this passage in Matthew 6:33. It is a reminder to be Kingdom focused. These are words to live by. Chase after the realm of the Kingdom of God and the righteousness that He has, and then all these lesser things will be abundantly given to you. We have to have Kingdom eyes if we are going to live the life God has planned for us. If you are viewing life through a natural, earthly perspective, it will suck you in and weigh you down every time.

Philippians 4:19-20 tells us that He satisfies every need according to His riches so He may be glorified. Isn't it remarkable that God gives us according to what He has instead of what we have or what our potential is? He wants you to have access to the Kingdom because it glorifies Him and will bring more people to Him.

> [19]" *I am convinced that my God will fully satisfy every need you have, for I have seen the abundant riches of glory revealed to me through the Anointed One, Jesus Christ!* [20] *And God our Father will receive all the glory and the honor throughout the eternity of eternities! Amen!*" Phil 4:19-20

The Kingdom of Heaven's response when we feel a lack in our lives is to press in and ask God to show us His nature and provision. God's nature is never to show you something you lack in life without also providing the solution. A great posture, to have before the Lord, is an openness to receive all that He has for you. With hands up and open wide, I guarantee what He wants to put in them will overflow.

When you think of T.P., be thankful that we are totally prosperous and not paranoid about where your provision comes from. We have an unshakable confidence because we know our identity and God has promised that we will prosper and excel in every season!

Because of the nature of Christ, this is our nature as well. We can hold to the promise in 1 Corinthians 15:57-58:

> [57] "But we thank God for giving us the victory as conquerors through our Lord Jesus, the Anointed One. So now, beloved ones, stand firm and secure. Live your lives with an unshakable confidence. We know that we prosper and excel in every **season** by serving the Lord because we are assured that our union with the Lord makes our labor productive with fruit that endures." 1 Corinthians 15:57-58

In turn, our response back to God:

> "Glorify God with all your wealth, honoring him with your very best, with every increase that comes to you. Then every dimension of your life will overflow with blessings from an uncontainable source of inner joy!" Proverbs 3:9-10

Lesson Learned

There is no lack in the Kingdom of God. We are totally prosperous in every season.

10. Ventilator

Just Breathe…God is your breath

2020 Observation

In 2020 during the pandemic, ventilators were the hot commodity in the medical needs. COVID-19 was a respiratory disease, and at first, ventilators were thought to be the solution to COVID-19. A ventilator is a machine that provides mechanical ventilation by moving breathable air into and out of the lungs to deliver breaths to a patient who is physically unable to breathe or breathing insufficiently.

Timeless Truth

Whenever stressful times come, we have trouble breathing. In fact, we seem to hold our breath. Have you ever seen or experience a panic attack coming on? A panic attack causes you to breathe heavier in an effort to catch your breath. For many of us, we just hold our breath when we are anxious. Have you found yourself doing this? I noticed it in my dad when he didn't feel well, he would be holding his breath. It was then I realized how often we hold our breath.

Whenever we are anticipating something, it seems like we are holding our breath, not completely shutting off oxygen, but enough to cut off life to our body. It often happens when we are waiting for something. This is where the saying came from, "Don't hold your breath!" It dates back to the 16th Century. Holding your breath is a natural reaction to an anxiety-provoking or stressful situation. So "don't hold your breath" assumes that the person being addressed will hold their breath in anticipation. Conversely, we let our sighs to restore our breathing. Even if you can't tell that someone is holding their breath, you may notice it when they let out a sigh.

The timeless truth is that we have difficulty breathing when we experience hard times. We are holding our breath and letting out sighs.

Kingdom Perspective

Breathing is a very Christian thing to do. God gives us our breath. Many times I think He is saying, "Just breathe." Our breath is a gift from God.

> *"Then the Lord God formed the man from the dust of the ground. He breathed the breath of life into the man's nostrils, and the man became a living person."* Genesis 2:7 (NLT)
>
> *"Here are the words of the true God, Yahweh, the one who created the starry heavens and stretched them out. He is the one who formed the earth and filled it with life. He gives breath to every person and spirit to everyone everywhere."* Isaiah 42:5

This idea of holding our breathing in anticipation of something really addresses worry. Whether we contracted COVID-19 or not, we were all holding our breath in anticipation of what the future might hold. We were all waiting to exhale in a sigh of relief that everything will be okay.

In the Kingdom of God, we know we cannot allow our outside circumstances to impact our Kingdom reality. In fact, when the storms of life come, we need to hold on tight and breathe. We can exhale during the storm because we know where our hope comes from. Jesus talked about worry and anxiety in Matthew 6. The instruction at the end of this passage was to refuse to worry about tomorrow. Don't you love that? Jesus is saying when someone offers you concern or worry, refuse it.

> *25 "This is why I tell you to never be worried about your life, for all that you need will be provided, such as food, water, clothing—everything your body needs. Isn't there more to your life than a meal? Isn't your body more than clothing?*
>
> *26 "Look at all the birds—do you think they worry about their existence? They don't plant or reap or store up food, yet your heavenly Father provides them each with food. Aren't you much more valuable to your Father than they? 27 So, which one of you by worrying could add anything to your life?*
>
> *28 "And why would you worry about your clothing? Look at all the beautiful flowers of the field. They don't work or toil, 29 and yet not even Solomon in all his splendor was robed in beauty more than one of these! 30 So if God has clothed the meadow with hay, which is here for such a short time and then dried up and burned, won't he*

> *provide for you the clothes you need—even though you live with such little faith?*
>
> [31] *"So then, forsake your worries! Why would you say, 'What will we eat?' or 'What will we drink?' or 'What will we wear?'* [32] *For that is what the unbelievers chase after. Doesn't your heavenly Father already know the things your bodies require?*
>
> [33] *"So above all, constantly chase after the realm of God's kingdom and the righteousness that proceeds from him. Then all these less important things will be given to you abundantly.* [34] *Refuse to worry about tomorrow, but deal with each challenge that comes your way, one day at a time. Tomorrow will take care of itself."* Matthew 6:25-33

Refuse to worry about tomorrow. How excellent is this instruction? We are to deal with the challenge that presents itself today and let tomorrow take care of itself. Ask yourself, how many things have you worried about that have actually come to pass? Have you taken today's forecast and extrapolated into tomorrow, next week, next month, next year, the next decade, etc.? We don't do that with the weather, we see it raining, and we don't say, what if this continues into tomorrow, then next week, then next month, what will we do? My sister first called this awfulizing. What a great phrase!

It is easy to tell someone to just breathe and much harder to do. How can we stay in the moment and not get outside the boundaries with today's problems? There are a couple of things we need to keep in mind and some other things we can do when we are triggered to worry. This starts with a relationship of trust with God. The discipline of staying present to the present and praying instead of worrying.

First and foremost, we have to remember that God takes care of us in every season. Read the first part of the Matthew 6 passage that tells us not to worry. Prior to this instruction on worry, Jesus is teaching about storing treasures in Heaven, because what we store here on earth is at risk. If you don't have an account with the Kingdom of God Savings and Trust Bank, it is time to get one. This can only be done by saying "yes" to Jesus and accepting Him as Lord and Savior.

Once you have this account with Jesus, which by the way, He has stocked it full of heavenly treasures, and we have full access to it, we can start making deposits of our own. Which means our time, talent, and resources needs to be invested with God. We need to understand the nature of who He is and the benefits we have because of our relationship with Him. Once we begin to trust Him, breathing easy in and out of difficult seasons becomes natural.

Many of us want our futures planned out, at least our near futures, and the unexpected idea is frightening. Ironically, many of us desire to change, but we don't want to change to get there. Being unsure of the unexpected and what that might mean gives many of us high anxiety and worry. We also tend to want to borrow trouble and extrapolate it into what that might mean for our future. Pretty soon, we are living in a less than ideal future, right now in the present.

It is so important to stay present to the present. What is happening right now? What do we need to get from today? What do we need to get from this lesson? Learning your lessons the first time around is preventative medicine for not having to experience it again, at least in the same way. As humans, we always tend to keep looking forward to the next thing. Take a minute, breathe, and really assess what this moment holds. Ask yourself some key questions:

- Am I safe right now?
- Do I have food?
- Are my loved ones safe?
- Do I have a roof over my head?
- What am I missing that causes fear for me to step out of this

moment?

That last question is key to how we pray. What am I missing? Father-God wants to supply what you are missing. These storms of life reveal the missing piece. That should give us enough confidence to welcome the storm because it is a direct correlation to God breathing more into us. In our storms, we uncover lack, and God supplies all of our needs. In all actuality, we should be celebrating the storms of our life because they signal an upgrade in what God has for us. Woohoo!

> [6] "*Don't be pulled in different directions or worried about a thing. Be saturated in prayer throughout each day, offering your faith-filled requests before God with overflowing gratitude. Tell him every detail of your life,* [7] *then God's wonderful peace that transcends human understanding, will make the answers known to you through Jesus Christ.*" Phil 4:6-7

Lesson Learned

Stay present to the present.

When you are in a fearful situation, stay present to the present, and just breathe! God is your breath and wants to give you more life.

"You will not be subject to terror, for it will not terrify you. Nor will the disrespectful be able to push you aside, Because God is your confidence in times of crisis, keeping your heart at rest in every situation." Proverbs 3:25-26

11. New Normal

See the Possibilities

2020 Observation

During the 2020 COVID-19 Pandemic, the nation went on lockdown. We were asked to shelter in place and only go out for essentials. This was supposed to last two weeks to allow medical facilities to prepare and to contain the virus. Depending on your state, the quarantine lasted from two weeks up to three months. It didn't take long for people to realize, life looked very different. The restrictions, in all likelihood, would not just lift, and everything returns to normal. There would have to be a "new normal."

Timeless Truth

What is normal? Normal is defined as the usual, average, or typical condition; that which is expected. The new normal also has a definition that is a previously unfamiliar or atypical situation that has become standard, usual, or expected.

Whenever something changes in our life, we experience a new normal. When a couple has been childless for years, she becomes pregnant and has a child. Their routine is changed and is now experiencing a new normal. Each stage of life of the child presents a new normal. From sleepless nights to teething, to walking, to potty training, to school, to puberty, to driving, to graduation, and off to college. We adapt to these changes.

The stark difference from the pandemic was that everything changed for everyone. It felt as if there was nothing to hold on to. This hadn't happened before in our life with what we had become accustomed to. Along with life changes, there is fear that can accompany the difference until we settle into our new normal. However, there is also a great opportunity that each shift in life presents.

Kingdom Perspective

As Christ-followers in the Kingdom of God, we are always looking for transformation or for change. We are told in Romans 12:2 to be transformed by the renewing of our minds. We work this out through teaching of God's word and demonstration of signs and wonders in some cases. There always seems to be a surprise when change happens to us, and we are not the agents of the change.

> *"Stop imitating the ideals and opinions of the culture around you, but be inwardly transformed by the Holy Spirit through a total reformation of how you think. This will empower you to discern God's will as you live a beautiful life, satisfying and perfect in his eyes."* Romans 12:2

As humans, we want to control the change or the rate of change which we will except. But many times change doesn't come about in digestible amounts. We get very uncomfortable when we see things shifting that are beyond our control. Fear rises up because we don't know how to deal with the problem at hand. We give in to anxiety, fear, and panic.

When storms of life hit us, we are always looking for something to hold on to. We are free-flowing down a rapid river grasping tree limbs or rocks. We are looking for something unchangeable to grab on to. What is something or someone we can count on? Every threat of change, if taken at face value, seems like a problem. It creates worry and anxiety because the life we knew is no longer available to us. Many of us will fight and complain until we get it back, we live as present-past people. Meaning, we are always looking backward to project the past into our future. When we can't do that, it causes great anxiety and worry.

With these changes, we have to come to grips that the future we painted for ourselves is now at risk. And in some cases, utterly unattainable with how we thought it might work out. Take someone who has lost a beloved spouse at a young age, the person they thought they would grow old with. Their future has been wiped clean and is now unknown. They thought they would travel together, watch their children grow up together, and be grandparents together. That future scenario is no longer available. Or maybe you have lost a career that you thought you would always be doing. Something you never saw yourself leaving, but things beyond your control changed.

As Christians, we are God's solution to helping humanity solve problems. If Christians are freaking out, then how is the world supposed to act? Let's look at problem-solving. When we look at issues through a lens of how do we solve the problem. There are four steps to problem-solving in the marketplace:

1. **Defining the problem.** It is essential to identify the problem and give it boundaries. Define what fact is and what is opinion.
2. **Generating alternatives.** Brainstorm

Problems are only opportunities in

work clothes. –
HENRY KAISER
(AMERICAN
INDUSTRIALIST)

alternatives to get to the desired result. Hold off on judging the ideas, there may be nuggets of truth and solutions in what at first glance seems crazy.

3. **Evaluating and selecting alternatives.** Look at the alternatives that you have listed. What makes sense to move forward with? Are there parts of a solution that may work. Don't throw the baby out with the bathwater.

4. **Implementing solutions.** Start applying the solutions. Be careful to not change too many things at once; you won't know how to evaluate which part of the solution worked or not.

This is a straight forward approach to problem-solving. The missing element is the emotions, and our feelings are not 100% trustworthy. While our senses can signify that there is a problem. They don't always identify those most immediate problems. There may be past experiences and unresolved issues that are influencing how we feel at this moment. Our feelings can lie to us if we don't make our feelings fall into alignment. This is not to suggest that we become cold and calculated, but that we put emotions into a proper perspective. Feelings cannot always be trusted.

So, how do we transition these four problem-solving steps into a Kingdom perspective? If we use this framework, we can see how we approach the problem through a Kingdom perspective and address our feelings along the way.

"We all experience times of testing, which is normal for every human being. But God will be faithful to you. He will screen and filter the severity, nature, and timing of

*every test or trial you face so that you can bear it. And each test is an **opportunity** to trust him more, for along with every trial God has provided for you a way of escape that will bring you out of it victoriously."* 1 Corinthians 10:13

1. **Defining the problem.**

What is the shift that seems to be happening? For some, there can be a feeling that something is happening or needs to change before it actually changes. Regardless, giving voice to the problem in prayer before God can be incredibly helpful. This is also a great time to share your feelings and let God separate the fact from opinion. There may be a feeling that you cannot put your finger on. You sense there is a change coming. Almost like the elderly person with hip replacement can tell you if it is going to rain. Let Father-God validate your feelings. He may want to give you insight further into what is coming.

When we pray with our problems, there is something we need to remember. That is the promise that God has given us. There is always a promise with comes with the problem. God put a rainbow in the sky with Noah because God is a God of promise. With every problem lies the promise of possibilities and provision. When things change beyond our control, Jesus is unchanging. Jesus is our firm foundation, our rock.

"Jesus, the Anointed One, is always the same—yesterday, today, and forever." Hebrews 13:8

2. Generating alternatives

The next step after recognizing the pain and defining the current problem is to discover options. Pray for understanding and a solution. Ask Father-God what He is doing and what you must do? Capture what the Holy Spirit brings to mind, feelings, visions, etc. Especially if they are things you would not think of. Pay attention to your dreams during this time. Also capture recurring themes from friends, both Christian and non-Christian. All of these things will help formulate options.

3. Evaluate and select alternatives

Many times the alternatives may not feel comfortable because they aren't from you; they are from God. He may be asking you to step out in this season. This isn't an invitation to do the crazy just for the sake of crazy, but it may be a season to do something on faith instead of fear.

Take each of your alternatives to God in prayer, there may not be many. Many times a solution is emerging that you sense is what God wants you to step into. At this point, start praying about the timing and who needs to be included in the solution.

4. Implementing solutions

The timing of implementation is crucial. Many times as Christians, we have the vision and can see what God is doing, and we have a tendency to get ahead of Him with implementing a solution. We don't want to waste the opportunity or release the promise, so it will be stolen before the timing is right. Think about the farmer. He may have great weather in January to put the seed in the field, but the timing isn't right. The weather would more than likely damage the seed, and his harvest would come up short.

5. Thanksgiving

This step has been included because coming to God with Thanksgiving is key before or after the solution. Before because we have the faith that God wants to be our provider or problem-solver and, of course, after because He has been faithful to finish what He has promised. As we move through these steps of prayer, there will be a couple of things you can expect.

First, the better we get at this, the quicker we will be able to turn the storms of life into opportunities and possibilities. Chances are the things we have been praying about, the answer lies within the storm. Step in quickly. Don't let the enemy get the opportunity to steal your promise.

> *"Lovers of God have been given eyes to see with spiritual discernment and ears to hear from God."*
> Proverbs 20:12

Second, the solution may come before the problem. What?!? It's true, many times God gets ahead of Himself, because yes He that good. He provides a solution before you experience the problem. Two examples come to mind with this current pandemic.

My friend, Laura, had an organization that fell apart a few years ago. It was painful and devastating. Her model for success depended on large gatherings. But just like Laura in her way, she stepped up and created a new model for her work. Two years before the pandemic, she rebuilt based on a smaller audience model and an online model. The pandemic became her harvest. How awesome is that? God had prepared her for this time before it happened. Her Plan B became her Plan A.

Our church started a year before the pandemic. Our numbers were so small, and we weren't able to grow. The beginning of the year led to some hard discussion and long looks at our model. We refigured our services and are planned shutdown for our Sunday Services were the same day the state-mandated that we shut down. The model we want to put in place fits more squarely with what the world is needing.

Third, God wants to call us friends. Not only does he wants to call us friends, but he wants to reveal more to us. Jesus tells us that we are called intimate friends when we obey all that He has commanded. Look at the promise in John 15, "I call you my most intimate friends, for I reveal to you everything that I've heard from the Father." So many times God will already be talking to you about the problem before it is revealed.

> ^{13} *For the greatest love of all is a love that sacrifices all. And this great love is demonstrated when a person sacrifices his life for his friends.*
>
> ^{14} *"You show that you are my intimate friends when you obey all that I command you. ^{15} I have never called you 'servants,' because a master doesn't confide in his servants, and servants don't always understand what the master is doing. But I call you my most intimate friends, for I reveal to you everything that I've heard from my Father.* John 15:13-15

Finally, God has a promise and provision available to us in problems. Your upgrade in life comes in the storm. We are now positioned to face storms with high expectations of a new normal. A new welcomed normal.

Learning Learned

There is promise, possibilities, and provision in every problem to create a new normal.

12. Essential Service

Church is an Essential Service

2020 Observation

What is an essential service? "Essential services" refers to those services vital to the health and welfare of a population and, therefore, essential to maintain even in a disaster. During the Global Pandemic, we heard a lot about what essential service was and what was not. Many churches had to close because they were not considered essential. Churches were closed through Easter Sunday of 2020. Most churches moved their weekly services online, and it was disappointing not to physically come together as the body of Christ.

Timeless Truth

Church attendance has been on the decline for decades. Many people have been calling church non-essential for years. Has the church lost its effectiveness?

Kingdom Perspective

Eighteen months ago, my husband, son, and I decided to launch a church in Springfield, IL. Our first weekly service was Easter of 2019. We struggled mightily the first year with attendance. People would come to check us out, give us kind words, and then rotate out. I believe it was more curiosity than a need for a new church. There is also a lot required of every person who becomes part of a new church start-up. I don't blame them, it is difficult. At the start of the second year, we were seeing some movement and excited for a great marketing campaign that was launching a month before Easter. Instead of a marketing campaign being launched, COVID-19 Pandemic was activated. The church was deemed non-essential, and we closed our physical doors. Great timing for a church, right?

If I was a fatalist, I would have been saying, "Of course, the church is non-essential, we decided to launch one. What else do you want to kill? I'm your girl!" Luckily, I'm not a fatalist. We could have very easily given up right then and there and pronounced it dead on arrival of COVID-19. One more COVID-19 death. But no, I'm an eternal optimist and asked God, "Where are you working now? Is this threat and opportunity for us that wouldn't have been available otherwise? Is our size actually an advantage?" So two and a half months later, we are re-launching on the Day of Pentecost.

Why didn't I give up? I love the church. I grew up in a small church in our little community in Loraine, IL. Our little Christian church was amazing. It helped form who I was and who I would become. I loved being at church, I loved hearing God's word preached, I loved the songs, and I loved the people. I love what Jesus has promised for the church. I have a desire to see her, the church, become everything Jesus intended. I want my children and grandchildren to experience what I have and more.

But, this next-generation church has to be better and more lovely and honoring then what we have become known for. It is time for the church, not just ours, to embrace their identity and destiny and come out swinging. Fighting the enemy for others; being advocates, treasure hunters, lovers, helpers, healers, basically the salt of the world.

Jesus died for the church, Paul's life and mission were for the church, the disciples all worked to spread the word and build the church. It doesn't matter what the public opinion is about the church. It doesn't matter what we have become. That is irrelevant. The only thing that matters is what God's plan is for her. What does God have planned for her? The first place Jesus mentions the church is in Matthew 16, after Peter's revelation from the Holy Spirit about Jesus' identity.

[13] *"When Jesus came to Caesarea Philippi, he asked his disciples this question: "What are the people saying about me, the Son of Man? Who do they believe I am?"*

[14] *They answered, "Some are convinced you are John the Baptizer, others say you are Elijah reincarnated, or Jeremiah, or one of the prophets."*

[15] *"But you—who do you say that I am?" Jesus asked.*

[16] *Simon Peter spoke up and said, "You are the Anointed One, the Son of the living God!"*

[17] *Jesus replied, "You are favored and privileged Simeon, son of Jonah! For you didn't discover this on your own, but my Father in heaven has supernaturally revealed it to you.* [18] *I give you the name Peter, a stone. And this truth of who I am will be the bedrock foundation on which I will build my church—my legislative assembly, and the power of death will not be able to overpower it!* [19] *I will give you the keys of heaven's kingdom realm to forbid on earth that which is forbidden in heaven, and to release on earth that which is released in heaven."* [20] *He then gave his disciples strict orders not to tell anyone that he was God's Anointed One."* Matthew 16:13-20

In The Passion Translation, the translator gives more description of the church. He uses 'legislative assembly.' The footnote in The Passion Translation for verse 18 is "The Greek word for "church" is *ekklesia* and means "legislative assembly" or "selected ones." This is not a religious term, but a political and governmental term used in classical Greek. Ekklesia was used to describe a people group summoned and gathered to govern a city's affairs. For Jesus to use this term means he is giving the keys of governmental authority in his Kingdom to the church."

The church or ekklesia is the legislative assembly for The Kingdom of God. We have been given the keys to the Kingdom. We have the authority to forbid on earth what has been forbidden in heaven, as well as release on earth what has been released in heaven. It is not only for leaders to be given this authority but for all of the church body.

Our church organizations should be training up leaders to have this authority and take it wherever they go. If we want to impact the world and be the assembly that Jesus was talking about, then the church cannot be a weekly obligation that makes us feel like we are on the right path. It has to be a training ground. The church is a safe place, not to get away from the world, but to train others for battling the enemy when we go to our home, our work, and our school.

Isaiah 61, which a portion of it is also in Luke 4, gives a job description for the church. Not just the collect church body but also for us as individuals who are the church. This was Jesus' mission, and he has positioned the church to carry it out to the end of the earth and until the end of time. Read and re-read Isaiah 61. If you don't know what your destiny is, this is it! This chapter will get you excited about church again. Take it to your church leaders and say we want to do this!

*The job description (based on Isaiah 61) of a churchman/
churchwoman is to:*

Requirements:

- understand the Holy Spirit is on us
- preach the good news to the poor
- heal the brokenhearted
- tell the captives, they are free
- tell prisoners to be free from their darkness
- comfort all who are in sorrow
- strengthen those who are crushed by depression
- encourage one another
- give a mantle of joyous praise instead of a spirit of heaviness

Title:

Priests of Yahweh

Because of the above is carried out, God will call you **"Mighty Oaks of Righteousness a living display of God's glory and The Priests of Yahweh."**

Project Goals:

- restore ruins from long ago
- rebuild what was long devastated
- renew ruined cities
- renew desolations of past generations

Benefits:

- Our daily chores will be taken care of
- We will feast with the wealth of nations
- Have riches
- We will be given a double portion of endless joy and bliss
- God will enter into an everlasting covenant with us (Jesus)

- Honor for us and our future generations
- Dressed with salvation and wrapped in righteousness
- Blossom before all nations

This is an excellent job description for the church. Many times we think the church is about the assembly, the building, or the leadership. The church is really about you, the Christ-follower. Your role as a church person is not to just go to church every time it is open, to give your offerings, to do your quiet times, to act right, and invite your neighbor to an event at the church. It is to be Christ-like in all you do!

But first, to be the church, we have to understand who we are in Christ. This life we live is so much more than a set of instructions. We are designed to live in relationship, relationship with the Father first. When we understand God's true nature and who He is and wants to be for us, it becomes easy to give it away to others.

To be the church is to live life. When we were locked down during COVID-19, there wasn't much living going on with each other. But it was a great chance to improve our relationship with the Father. No time is wasted in the Kingdom. We should continuously be working on our relationships. The way the Father deals with us is to love us and show us areas where we lack, then give us what we require. This is what we should model, as well. Love on others, show them where God has revealed what you lack in life and how He has filled it, then give it away so they can build their relationship. Father-God wants to do life with us, and we, in turn, do life with others while remaining in Him. This is how we evangelize the world through our relationships. When we uncover needs, we bring them before God.

Isaiah 61 in its entirety:

1 *"The mighty Spirit of Lord Yahweh is wrapped*
around me

because Yahweh has anointed me,

as a messenger to preach good news to the poor.

He sent me to heal the wounds of the brokenhearted,
to tell captives, "You are free,"
and to tell prisoners, "Be free from your darkness."
2 *I am sent to announce a new season of Yahweh's grace*
and a time of God's recompense on his enemies,
to comfort all who are in sorrow,
3 *to strengthen those crushed by despair who mourn in*
Zion—
to give them a beautiful bouquet in the place of ashes,
the oil of bliss instead of tears,
and the mantle of joyous praise
instead of the spirit of heaviness.
Because of this, they will be known as
Mighty Oaks of Righteousness,
planted by Yahweh as a living display of his glory.
4 *They will restore ruins from long ago*
and rebuild what was long devastated.
They will renew ruined cities
and desolations of past generations.
5 *Foreigners will be appointed to shepherd your many*
flocks;
strangers will cultivate your fields and tend your vines.

6 *But you will be known as Priests of Yahweh,*
and called Servants of our God.
You will feast on the wealth of nations

It is essential to understand that the church is a paradox. It is a building, and it is the people. When the governmental authorities shut down churches, they shut down the building, not the people. Whether we have a building or not, we will always be essential. If you ever have any doubt, look to the cross. The value of something is placed on what someone is willing to pay for it. Jesus paid it all. Jesus sacrificed and died for the church, and God will always have the final word.

We may not always be able to worship the way we are accustomed to, but we still worship. In Hebrews 10:24, it tells us to discover creative ways to encourage others. But verse 25 also reminds us not to neglect meeting together because we need each other. In fact, the verse encourages us to meet even more frequently. The Holy Spirit will always provide the way forward for the church. Let's give thanks for this season as Father-God is breathing new life into us, the church.

> ^{24} Discover creative ways to encourage others and to motivate them toward acts of compassion, doing beautiful works as expressions of love. ^{25} This is not the time to pull away and neglect meeting together, as some have formed the habit of doing because we need each other! In fact, we should come together even more frequently, eager to encourage and urge each other onward as we anticipate that day dawning."
>
> Hebrews 10:24-25

CHURCH – LET OUR LIGHT SHINE!

As Christ-followers, we are the church and we will always be essential to advancing the Kingdom of God and glorifying God here on earth.

Hope of Glory

[26] "*that is, the mystery which has been hidden from the past ages and generations, but has now been manifested to His saints,* [27] *to whom God willed to make known what is the riches of the glory of this mystery among the Gentiles, which is Christ in you, the hope of glory.*" Colossians 1:26-27 (NASB)

Salt of the Earth

[13] "*Your lives are like salt among the people. But if you, like salt, become bland, how can your 'saltiness' be restored? Flavorless salt is good for nothing and will be thrown out and trampled on by others.* Matthew 5:13

Light to the World

[14] "*Your lives light up the world. Let others see your light from a distance, for how can you hide a city that stands on a hilltop?* [15] *And who would light a lamp and then hide it in an obscure place? Instead, it's placed where everyone in the house can benefit from its light.* [16] *So don't hide your light! Let it shine brightly before others so that the commendable things you do will shine as light upon them, and then they will give*

their praise to your Father in heaven."
Matthew 5:14-16

13. First Responder

Jesus is our First Responder

2020 Observation

A **first responder** is a person with specialized training who is among the first to arrive and provide assistance at the scene of an emergency, such as an accident, natural disaster, or terrorism.[1] During COVID-19, there were requests for first responders, basically anyone in the medical field that could help out during this time. Hot spot areas, like New York City, New Orleans, and Chicago, needed more than rural America. About a month later, many medical professionals were furloughed because the perceived demand was greater than actual needs.

Timeless Truth

In troubled times, there is always a need for first responders, those willing to be first on the scene to help out. When storms in life come, we take on one of the three roles; victim, bystander, or first responder. Victims can be those who are actually impacted or those who fear they will be affected. A bystander basically has a 'wait and see' attitude. They are willing to watch it play out. The first

1. https://en.wikipedia.org/wiki/First_responder

responder is the one who is willing and feels called to rush in. First responders look beyond their own well-being to those who are impacted. Which role do you play?

Kingdom Perspective

As church leaders, it seems like we are working with victims or bystanders. Those who have been hurt or those who are trying to avoid being hurt. We encourage our congregations that God is in control, to keep the faith and Jesus is coming back soon, just hold on. My husband likes to refer to this as "hangin' on by your fingertips Christianity." We rarely believe it is our responsibility as leaders to take victims and bystanders and train them up to be first responders. However, if Jesus is our model for Christian behavior, then that is exactly what we should be doing. When we find our identity in Christ, we come to discover the first responder role is in our job description.

It is the nature of the trinity to be a first responder. Jesus called Father-God his first responder when He was hanging on the cross. You may not remember that because it was subtle. In Matthew 27:46, we see where Jesus called out to God from the cross, "My God, My God, why have you deserted me?" This line is the start of Psalm 22, and the Psalm ends with it is finished. The Psalm is a prophetic word from King David, prophesying the events of the cross. Within this Psalm, the translator of The Passion Translation uses "first responder" to describe the Father. Jesus and the Psalmist, David, give us insight into the nature of the Father. He is our first responder.

> ^{23} *"Lovers of Yahweh, praise him!*
> *Let all the true seed of Jacob glorify him with your*
> *praises.*
> *Stand in awe of him, all you princely people,*
> *the offspring of Israel!*
> ^{24} *For he has not despised my cries of deep despair.*
> *He's my **first responder** to my sufferings,*
> *and he didn't look the other way when I was in pain.*
> *He was there all the time, listening to the song of the*
> *afflicted.*
> ^{25} *You're the reason for my praise; it comes from you*
> *and goes to you."*   Psalm 22:23-25

Jesus also proves to be a fantastic first responder. He comes on the scene to save a hurting world. Jesus was the first one to usher in the Kingdom of God and demonstrate what it was like to live in the Kingdom. He healed the sick, raised the dead, gave sight to the blind, and gave hope to a desperate oppressed world. Jesus modeled for us the way to be a first responder. He demonstrated to the disciples how to step in when no one else will or knows how. Jesus called the disciples to be first responders, but He also calls us into the field.

Stepping out into the world in times of trouble, when no one else is, is risky. We have to risk our comfort and our reputation. This works best when we understand our identity as well as our position in the Kingdom. Hopefully, the previous chapters have given you insight into what that looks like. Our faith is a gift. Not just a gift that we can rest easy and sleep at night, but our faith is what allows us to step out. And to step out in a way that brings hope and life to desperate situations. To breathe life back into those who are holding their breath. Your salvation is not just a ticket to Heaven, it is a calling to step up and out and share with others. The great news is that we are not alone.

The third person of the trinity, the Holy Spirit, is also a first responder, and He is brilliant. The Holy Spirit's very nature is a first responder. Holy Spirit is amazing at letting us know when things happen even before we see them, and some times before they happen. He is brilliant at preparing the way. The Holy Spirit not only points out where the emergency is but also brings the knowledge and understanding of how to handle it. He is the best emergency response vehicle there is. If your life isn't overflowing with the spirit, it is time for an upgrade in your new creation self. Take a moment and pray for the Holy Spirit to fill you up.

During the pandemic, there was an alert that went out over our phones. It was a plea for medical professionals, those who were retired from the field, to return to help out with the COVID-19 pandemic. Immediately, I thought I'm not qualified for this. I'm sure I could help, but I may be getting in the way of the real professionals. Many of us do not feel qualified to be first responders to the world. What are the qualities of a first responder? A search online will provide many lists of what it means to be a first responder in today's world. With the help of the Holy Spirit, here is a list that I came up with:

- Listener
- Courage
- Compassion
- Understanding
- Intermediary
- Healer

Some may look at this list and think, "I have a couple of these, but not all of them." I'm not qualified to be a first responder in this world. Before you discount yourself, you are qualified. Romans 8:16-17 tells us that we are children of God, joint-heirs with Jesus, and we are positioned to inherit all of his treasures. You may have thought about these verses as what you inherit but not what you are qualified for. Our Kingdom position begins the day we say "yes" to Jesus. This is where the shift in mindset needs to take place.

Many of us know we don't need to work our way to Heaven, but I better be doing something that looks like work. We have a difficult time laying down our performance. Our mind needs to make the switch, we don't have to do anything for the Kingdom. However, as sons and daughters, we get to. In fact, in John 14:12-14, Jesus tells the disciples that we are too, we will do greater miracles than He did. Whatever we ask in His name. It would be a shame to not use our identity and God's abilities and willingness to help the world.

> [16] "*For the Holy Spirit makes God's fatherhood real to us as he whispers into our innermost being, "You are God's beloved child!"*
>
> [17] *And since we are his true children, we qualify to share all his treasures, for indeed, we are heirs of God himself. And since we are joined to Christ, we also inherit all that he is and all that he has. We will experience being co-glorified with him provided that we accept his sufferings as our own."* Romans 8:16-17
>
> ---
>
> [12] *"I tell you this timeless truth: The person who follows me in faith, believing in me, will do the same mighty miracles that I do—even greater miracles than these because I go to be with my Father!*[13] *For I will do whatever you ask me to do when you ask me in my name. And that is how the Son will show what the Father is really like and bring glory to him.*[14] *Ask me anything in my name, and I will do it for you!"* John 14:12-14

What is our job description? What are we to do? Do what Jesus did? Sit up straight, shoulders back, and notice who around you is hurting.

> [18] *Then Jesus came close to them and said, "All the authority of the universe has been given to me.*[19] *Now go in my authority and make disciples of all nations, baptizing them in the name of the Father, the Son, and the Holy Spirit.*[20] *And teach them to faithfully follow all that I have commanded you. And never forget that I am with you every day, even to the completion of this age."*
> Matthew 28:18-19

Step in and listen. Listening to the Kingdom is very different than in the world. Personally, I am not a great listener when more than one person is talking. However, as a first responder, we must learn this skill. Keeping our ears tuned to the person in front of you while listening to the Holy Spirit. The Holy Spirit is incredible at filling in the gaps of what the person is not saying, letting you know their true feelings, and then strategically giving you the words to say and the actions that should go with it.

Give an encouraging word. Proverbs 25:11-12 tells us about the right word spoken at the right time can change a person's heart. The translator of The Passion Translation made a footnote to verse 11 that says, "When we are full of his Spirit we can speak and prophesy words of encouragement that are spoken at the right time for the blessing of others."

> [11] *"Winsome words spoken at just the right time*
> *are as appealing as apples gilded in gold*
> *and surrounded with silver.*
> [12] *To humbly receive wise correction*
> *adorns your life with beauty*
> *and makes you a better person."*
>
> Proverbs 25:11-12

I didn't always have the best view of encouragement. Growing up in church, it felt like encouragement was more of a way to gloss over the real problem and shame people into acting right because, "Hey we're Christians, we should be happy. And if you're not happy, you should just get over it." Father-God corrected my opinion on encouragement. Many people kept speaking that I was an encourager and that I would be a great encourager as well. It was all I could do to hold in, nope, not me. I'm the real deal, if something stinks, then I'm going to be authentic and say it stinks. I'm too honest to be an encourager.

Holy Spirit showed me that wasn't what He meant by encouragement. He gently guided my thinking into how I process things. He was telling me to break down the word. This makes sense in my world because I am a word person. I like words, the meaning of words, plays on words, being clear in your speech, because words create worlds. Anyway, I broke down encouragement. Holy Spirit was bouncing up and down saying, do you see it? The word courage. I could just see, in my imagination, the Holy Spirit saying, "What Father-God is trying to show you is you are placing courage inside of people by sharing who He is. The nature of God brings courage to others. I am courage-in-you." Oh my gosh, that is amazing and makes sense. Let's be encouragers and wake people up to who God is in them. Yes! I can do that. Will you?

We also need a heart for others. Not just the down and out, but also the obstinate. This will take a lot of Holy Spirit to work in us. But He is faithful. Our prayers can be, *"Father, please break our hearts for people. Show us your compassion and how you love them. My love is insufficient, I need yours. I need a heart for understanding."* I believe Father-God loves this prayer. He loves it because we want His heart, and He wants to give it to us. As believers, children of God, we are looking more and more like our Father in Heaven. How exciting!

The last attribute is the riskiest. Our willingness to pray for others. Many of us are great at advice, and we think that if we bring our best self to the table, those receiving our greatness should be most thankful. However, that model is exhausting and has its limitations. The best thing we can do for others is to put ourselves aside and being willing to usher people into the throne room of Jesus. We need to get used to saying, "Can I pray for you right now?" They will probably be shocked, but most will say yes.

Invite the Holy Spirit into the prayer and ask Him to show us how to pray, how to comfort, and what are the next steps. This removes the pressure to have an answer for every situation, while at the same time demonstrates to the one receiving prayer how to pray when you are not there.

Some may say yes but say they aren't Christians. You can let them know it is not required for God to be good and help out, but you are also willing to take care of that. You can ask them if they would like to accept Jesus as their Lord and Savior. If yes, then just help them ask Jesus into their hearts. Once you are done praying, you can say that God is available at any time to answer their prayers.

We should not be surprised if something happens. If people feel better, spirits are lifted, bodies are healed, provision is realized, and the Kingdom expands. Don't be surprised if you experience joy and healing as well. You have thrown them a lifeline that will work in and out of every storm that comes. You have demonstrated what it means to put your faith in the one who can make all things possible. You are the first responder!

Lesson Learned

The Kingdom of God is looking for first responders. As Christians, we are incredibly created and fully equipped to rush in and be the first responder to the world. Who will answer the call?

14. Re-Open

Before You Step Out, Test Positive For Faith

2020 Observation

During the 2020 COVID-19 pandemic, people were encouraged to test if they showed signs of the disease. If they tested positive, then there were to follow The Center for Disease Control (CDC) guidelines, which included isolating yourself from others. It was recommended that you stay in your own room at home if you have tested positive, so you wouldn't infect your family members.

Timeless Truth

Any threat is a test of our faith and how God will take care of us in times of difficulty. Our faith is tested whether it is a global pandemic, an isolated disease, a natural disaster, or relational strife.

Kingdom Perspective

What is faith? Dictionary.com tells us it is complete confidence in someone or something. The Bible says to us in Hebrews 11:1, *"Now faith brings our hopes into reality and becomes the foundation needed to acquire the things we long for. It is all the evidence required to prove what is still unseen."*

Are we ready to step on in faith? How do we test our faith? Let's take a quiz.

When things are going well, where is your worry?

√ Finances – I am concerned there will not be enough to make ends meet.

√ Health – I am concerned you I won't be able to take care of yourself.

√ Family – I am concerned about my family, and I don't know what to do.

√ Future – Future? What is a future? I don't know how today will unfold.

√ Relationships – To be honest, I am lonely. No one understands me, and people don't like me.

Which ones of these do you worry about? What do you find yourself thinking about with no solutions coming forward? Which ones feel out of your control? Anything keeping you up at night?

Conversely, where is your complete confidence? Something you never worry about.

√ Finances – I have enough money and a steady stream of income. I've got this!

√ Health – I am the picture of health. I eat right, exercise, and stay away from bad things.

√ Family – My family is good. They are confident, and I am not worried.

√ Future – I have a life plan, I am checking things off and meeting my goals and milestones.

√ Relationships – Wow! Do I have friends! I also am married to the love of my life!

If you see yourself in any of the above scenarios, you are at risk. That may have just thrown you into a tailspin. Even if you tested positive for all of the latter categories, you are still at risk. You may be frustrated that you read this entire book, and now I am telling you that you failed the faith test. Before you throw the book into the fire or delete it permanently from your e-reader, let me explain.

The above 10 statements are all the same. They are all based on a snapshot in time. If anything changes, then you may go from worried to confident or confident to worried. If you are basing your answers on how you feel now, then you aren't ready to step out in faith. Remember, faith isn't about how much you have; it is about where you place it. If you put your faith in any of these buckets because of your ability, experience, position, stage of life, or anything that is manmade, you, my friend, are at risk. You are vulnerable to the enemy and the instability of others.

However, if you have just a mustard seed of faith placed in God for each of these. You are ready to move forward and step out in faith. Jesus taught about the mustard seed in Matthew 13 and 17. In Matthew 13, he talks about how small the seed is but the potential it holds. In Matthew 17, Jesus is talking with the disciples about faith after they failed to drive out a demon. He attributed the failure to their lack of faith. If they would just have a mustard seed of faith, they could move mountains. I would think the disciples would have more than a mustard seed of faith because they saw Jesus perform miracles. Their faith wasn't about how much they had, but who they placed it in and that God was willing to work through them. They had faith God would work through Jesus, but how about us?

We know that God is able to supply all our needs, but we aren't confident that He is willing. Jesus answers the willingness to bring Kingdom breakthrough when He heals the leper. Read this account in Luke 5.

> *¹² One day, while Jesus was ministering in a certain city, he came upon a man covered with leprous sores. When the man recognized Jesus, he fell on his face at*

> *Jesus' feet and begged to be healed, saying, "If you are only*
> *willing, you could completely heal me."*
>
> ¹³⁻¹⁴ *Jesus reached out and touched him and said, "Of*
> *course I am willing to heal you, and now you will be*
> *healed." Instantly the leprous sores were healed and his*
> *skin became smooth.*   Luke 5:12-14

The leper knew Jesus was able, but he didn't have faith in Jesus' willingness. Jesus put the leper's mind at ease and reassured him and then healed him. God wants us to have the same access that Jesus does to His authority and all the blessings of the Kingdom. When we mistrust the Father and His nature, we rob ourselves of the grace of the Kingdom.

> **Verses to meditate on for more hope:**
>
> "But those who hope in the Lord will renew their strength. They will soar on the wings like eagles; they will run and not grow weary, they will walk and not be faint." Isaiah 40:31
>
> "Be strong and courageous. Do not be afraid or terrified because of them, for the Lord your God goes with you; he will never leave you nor forsake you." Deuteronomy 31:6
>
> "Surely the righteous will never be shaken; they will be remembered forever. They will have no fear of bad news; their hearts are steadfast, trusting in the Lord.

Their hearts are secure, they will have no fear; in the end, they will look in triumph on their foes." Psalm 112:6-8

"For the Spirit God gave us does not make us timid, but gives us power, love and self-discipline." 2 Timothy 1:7

The Kingdom of God is all about faith. It is bringing the unseen into the seen. When we understand how the Kingdom works then, we realize the importance of faith. Faith is also a gift from the Holy Spirit. Have you ever had an experience where you just knew something would happen? You didn't have any facts, but you had a "gut feeling." Those gut feelings are a gift from the Holy Spirit; it is the gift of faith. We don't always experience those in the Kingdom realm, sometimes we know it in our head because we have seen it before, and we know God's goodness. The resolve is gone, so hope kicks in. But we still always have a faith for the Kingdom advancing.

Faith is the foundation needed to acquire abundant living that Jesus spoke of in John 10. If we lack faith, then our foundation is weak. Before we are ready to step out into the world and into life's difficulties, we need to have our faith tested. Testing positive for faith allows us to step forward into life's challenges with confidence in a new normal, with confidence that God has us safe, with a confidence that we are made to face our storms not run for them, and with a confidence that we may be the voice in the crowd saying 'quiet.'

If we test negative for faith, then we need to retreat into the shelter of the Most High. You aren't disqualified, you have just uncovered the areas that need to be surrendered to God. There is a risk if we intermingle our lack of faith or fear with others who lack faith. Our fear will grow into a bigger problem, and we will become toxic to others. James tells us if our faith remains strong during life's difficulties, we will experience untold blessings.

> "If your faith remains strong, even while surrounded by life's difficulties, you will continue to experience the untold blessings of God! True happiness comes as you pass the test with faith, and receive the victorious crown of life promised to every lover of God!" James 1:12

Faith will grow through stories. When we hear or read how God has worked with others in life's difficulties, our hope is restored. We can be confident that He is willing and able to do it for you if He did it for someone else.

Building up faith in others:

Hebrews 11 is a famous book in the Bible. It is the Bible Hall of Fame if you will. *"This testimony of faith is what previous generations were commended for. Faith empowers us to see that the universe was created and beautifully coordinated by the power of God's words! He spoke and the invisible realm gave birth to all that is seen."* (Hebrews 11:2-3) We can join that Hall of Fame when we step out in faith. Let's look at a few, but you are encouraged to read it for yourself.

- Faith moved Abel to chose a more acceptable sacrifice (v.4)
- Faith lifted Enoch from this life into heaven (v.5)
- Faith opened Noah's heart to receive revelation (v.7)
- Faith motivated Abraham (the father of stepping out in faith) to obey God's call and leave the familiar (v.8)
- Faith embraced by Sarah resulted in a miraculous conception, past the childbearing age (v.11)
- Faith operated powerfully in Abraham to be tested to offer Isaac as a sacrifice (v.17)
- Faith prompted Isaac to impart a blessing to his sons concerning their destinies (v.19)

- Faith's reality was achieved through Jacob's faith, who gave a prophetic blessing to Joseph's sons. (v.21)
- Faith inspired Joseph to open his eyes to see the future about the exodus of Israel. (v.22)
- Faith prompted Moses' parents to hide him at birth, and they refused to be afraid of the king's edict (v.23)
- Faith enabled Moses to choose God's will, preferring faith's certainty to momentary pleasures (v. 24)
- Faith's persistence enabled Moses to have no fear of Pharaoh's rage (v.27)
- Faith stirred Moses to perform the rite of Passover and sprinkle lamb's blood, to prevent the destroyer from harming their firstborn. (v.28)
- Faith opened the way for the Hebrews to cross the Red Sea as if on dry land, but when the Egyptians tried to cross, they were swallowed up and drowned! (v.29)
- Faith pulled down Jericho's walls after the people marched around them for seven days! (v.30)
- Faith provided an escape for Rahab, avoiding the destruction of the unbelievers because she received the Hebrew spies in peace. (v.31)
- Faith's power conquered kingdoms and established true justice. (v.33)
- Faith fastened onto their promises and pulled them into reality! (v.33)

Many others are mentioned in this passage and throughout history. Without faith living within us, it is impossible to please God. These heroes died clinging to their faith and changing the world. When we get faith at the levels being offered, the unseen will become more logical than the seen. Abraham believed it was logical for God to raise Isaac from the dead before he sacrificed him. He had so much faith in God's promise that logic took over. Have you ever asked yourself how Abraham could go through with God's request of sacrificing his only child? It was because his faith was so great that faith turned into logic. When we can see the ultimate reality instead of the immediate, we know our faith is Kingdom strong, and that is faith's great reward. That is powerful!

Let's retake this quiz from putting our mustard seed faith in Father-God and knowing His willingness to provide for us.

√ Finances – I am confident that the Lord will bring me my daily bread and provide for me according to His riches. (Phil 4:19)

√ Health – Jesus is my Healer, and God is my breath. I am weak, but God is strong. (2 Cor. 12:9)

√ Family – I will be a Father to you, and you will be my sons and daughters. (2 Cor. 6:8, Acts 16:31, Ps. 112:1-2)

√ Future – God has a plan for my future. (Jer. 29:11)

√ Relationships – Nothing will separate us from the love of God. (Rom. 8:38-39)

When you can answer this way for these, you are ready to step out in faith.

Lesson Learned

"For we live by faith, not by what we see with our eyes"

[6] *"That's why we're always full of courage. Even while we're at home in the body, we're homesick to be with the Master—* [7] ***for we live by faith, not by what we see with our eyes.*** [8] *We live with joyful confidence, yet at the same time, we take delight in the thought of leaving our bodies behind to be at home with the Lord.* [9] *So whether we live or die we make it*

²¹*My child, never drift off course from these two goals for your life:*
to walk in wisdom and to discover discernment.
Don't ever forget how they empower you.
²² *For they strengthen you inside and out*
and inspire you to do what's right;
you will be energized and refreshed by the healing they bring.
²³ *They give you living hope to guide you,*
and not one of life's tests will cause you to stumble.
²⁴ *You will sleep like a baby, safe and sound—*
your rest will be sweet and secure.
²⁵ *You will not be subject to terror, for it will not terrify you.*
Nor will the disrespectful be able to push you aside,
²⁶ *because God is your confidence in times of crisis,*
keeping your heart at rest in every situation.
Proverbs 3:21-26

15. Last Thought

There is one more nuance that needs to be addressed when it comes to vulnerability. Again, COVID-19 impacted the entire world but not equally. It wasn't equal because our weaknesses aren't the same. Interestingly enough, this resulted in more fighting and polarization of people. I'm not sure this was the enemy's plan, but it played into lots of division. Our vulnerability puts us at risk for how we relate to each other. If your vulnerability isn't the same as mine, then the solution you choose could step harder on my vulnerability. For example, with the current pandemic, if my vulnerability is health and fear of death, then a nationwide quarantine makes sense. If my vulnerability is financial security and fear of loss of income or economic stability, then going back to work and opening up businesses makes sense. These two opposing vulnerabilities put us at odds.

We don't all process fear the same way. No matter where you are on your journey, remember to be compassionate and kind to others. My vulnerabilities are not the same as yours. My conviction for what needs to be done will also be different than yours. Let's be aware of how a common or uncommon threat can impact us differently. Work hard at understanding your neighbor.

About Carla Green

Carla Green is an author, pastor, strategist, grandmother, mother, wife, and child of God. She loves seeing where God is working in all situations. Carla is Kingdom-minded and has a passion for seeing more Kingdom breakthrough in her home, work, neighborhood, and city. She loves to make people laugh and has a unique view of words. Carla enjoys spending time with her family and friends.

www.ingramcontent.com/pod-product-compliance
Lightning Source LLC
Chambersburg PA
CBHW051425150726
48000CB00005B/1965